Relationship

Advice

2 Books in 1: How to Be the King of Dating, Sex, Relationship, and Marriage with Secret Tips to Seduce the Love of Your Life and Keep Him or Her for Forever

Samantha Gilbert

Relationship

Advice

How to Be the King of Dating, Sex, Relationship, and Marriage with Secret Tips to Seduce the Love of Your Life and Keep Him or Her for Forever

Part-1

Samantha Gilbert

Table of Contents

Relationship

Advice

How to Be the King of Dating, Sex, Relationship, and Marriage with Secret Tips to Seduce the Love of Your Life and Keep Him or Her for Forever

Part-2

Samantha Gilbert

Table of Contents

Relationship Advice

to date, and reliable, complete information. No warranties of any kind are declared or implied. Readers acknowledge that the author is not engaging in the rendering of legal, financial, medical or professional advice. The content within this book has been derived from various sources. Please consult a licensed professional before attempting any techniques outlined in this book.

By reading this document, the reader agrees that under no circumstances is the author responsible for any losses, direct or indirect, which are incurred as a result of the use of information contained within this document, including, but not limited to, — errors, omissions, or inaccuracies.

Relationship Advice

INTRODUCTION

Have you been looking for love in all the wrong places and in too many faces; only to find more pain and despair?

Then it is time to find out the truth regarding your search for true love.

You don't need to engage in an endless search for Mr. or Mrs. Right, nor do you settle or compromise for any Mr. or Mrs. Right now. If you continue to search for Mr. or Mrs. Right you will inevitably lose yourself trying to please others who can never really be pleased.

When you engage in trying to satisfy the unappeasable you are doing nothing more than giving them the power to control your life. Of course the powerful one is the subtle redeemer of all your good deeds, and can effortlessly play the game all day long everyday. It's much more important to empower yourself by knowing where your love really exists, than it is to be drained of your energy or continue to feel betrayed and end up abandoned by continually giving to someone who is not giving back to

13

you.

Instead of surviving in the lack of love where you find yourself alone, you turn your precious love and attention towards the person who most deserves it, you! So that you can become very consciously aware of any inner healing that is necessary to occur within you that has caused you to invest so much of yourself without any returns.

True Love is the remembrance and moment-to-moment application and expression of self-love. This honors the value of you, your divine magnificence.

You will want to attend to you to be sure you eliminate anything inside of you that is causing you to attract those outer relationships that are less than honorable, respectful and loving. Your healing can occur quickly; as when you are engaged in paying attention to the true love of self, your heart opens and is willing to receive.

The difficulty for most in accepting and acknowledging their own true love is due to the painful experiences from past lives and the past in this life. These experiences are encoded on a cellular level within you. You fear being fully open with your freedom of expression of self on all levels, not just due to the old painful experiences, but at the real causal level originating from when you first chose to lower your vibration to digress into matter, human form when you subscribed to incorrectly believing you are unworthy of true love.

When you incarnate, you came in with a veil of forgetfulness. You are not conscious of this veil, and thusly, you sense a separation from your source, God/Goddess.

In human form you have an ego, or the lower mental mind. This lower mental mind does not have the capacity of understanding like the universal higher mind does. The lower mind attempts to calculate and figure everything out rather than simply connecting to the inner feelings of love.

The lower mind attempting to figure out the sensation of separation, reasons that you must have done something wrong, and your abandonment is a direct punishment for your incorrectly perceived crime. The ego doesn't remember that your soul made the choice to simply experience incarnation for the very purpose of realizing the love it truly is.

Thusly, it calculates if you have done wrong you must be penalized for your wrong doing in some manner. You engage in one life experience after another punishing self in one form or another for doing nothing more than choosing life on earth.

These self-abusing experiences accumulate and compound as you continue to cycle through this incorrect belief of wrong doing punishable by whatever. What you are really unconsciously doing is creating one opportunity after another to be able to see the higher truth of being your own true love. Unfortunately, you as well as many have been stuck in this unhealthy behavior for eons

The self-punishment does have a silver lining, as a result of your multiple painful experiences, you can realize the greater truth that states you have done no wrong, the truth that states you can do no wrong because you are and have always been love. Love that is creating many experiences to realize it is love personified.

The time is now, as this is the Golden age of Heaven on Earth, where all will come to realize the truth of the true love of self.

You need not wait for anyone else to shift your incorrect beliefs into divine knowingness, nor do you need to fear them any longer. For those whom are still not ready to fully awaken to the truth will not be able to get any where near you once you choose love. When you are connected to your true love, you will not encounter these souls, as you have in the past; who are choosing to live in a lower vibration and are stuck in treating others badly because they don't value themselves to begin with.

You need not fear being vulnerable and walking with an open heart, as those who have not yet learned to love themselves simply will not cross your path. The energy of love is a far greater frequency and nothing vibrating from fear will be able to get any where near you. Love cannot encounter fear and those players who are stuck in fear will be on different grounds where they will continue to have the necessary less than loving experiences, so they can come to the same realization of remembering they were never lacking love and need not steal it from another.

When you incorrectly believe you are lacking love, you seek outside of yourself, another person, place or thing that will fulfill and satisfy this sense of lacking. You continue to pursue others one after the other in search of the love you are not willing to give yourself. Sometimes you may play the role of the victim by giving and never receiving equally in return, or you might take on the opposing role of the abuser, where you constantly take without ever being satisfied.

When you play the victim you give anyone and/or everyone the credits for your feel goods and you also project the blame for your feel bads. When you are the abuser you simply blame everyone for everything therefore righteously licensing your terrible treatment of others.

The ego is insatiable because it thrives on the sense of lack; lack is what fuels its fires and thusly you give the power to the ego of self, in your endless search of another to fulfill the very love of which you already are.

Until you are willing, as you have always been able, to stay and master the ego and its control over you and your life by realizing you are responsible for all the choices you have made; you will never come to know and live in the bliss of true love.

Your true love is you!

It does not exist outside of you. The one that exists outside of you is known more commonly as, the conscious life partner or twin flame. Although you will never enjoy the benefits of this whole relationship either until you realize your wholeness lies within.

How could you expect a whole individual to desire to live with and stand by the side of one who believes they are half a person, or lesser than. It simply cannot occur because the vibratory rates are completely different.

The whole individual is vibrating with a frequency of abundance of love of self and therefore lacks nothing. This individual needs no one, even though they may choose to share their life with another. The half individual perceives they are in lack and therefore is always needy. The half person lives in fear and the whole person lives in love, as stated above love and fear simply cannot encounter one another.

You have already experienced the kind of relationship when two fearful low vibrating individuals get together. These two are like separate halfs attempting to make a whole. They may be very attracted at first, because they are both looking for the same thing, someone to make them whole. Eventually they will unconsciously battle over control of the whole. Often with each half switching roles flipping back and forth from the powerful controlling one to the submissive one.

When you incorrectly believe that you lack something and then engage in attempts to fulfill yourself outside of yourself, you will experience being surrounded by many who seem to not want to give you the time of day. They dismiss your opinion as if it is worthless and they don't return the love you wish to give or have given to them.

Anyone one who believes they are not fulfilled without the other half is holding a lower vibration and cannot realize true love until they heal their incorrect beliefs about being less than love, less than loving, less than lovable and less than loved.

Opposing energies cannot meet and stay together for an extended period of time unless one or both change to vibrate at the same rate of frequency. The higher vibrational person will never encounter the lower vibrational individual unless they are participating in their lives for the purpose of healing. In as such the relationship is only temporary unless the lower vibratory person raises its frequency to love and/or the higher vibratory person lowers it frequency to fear.

You will not realize and walk side by side with that life partner or twin flame and/or peers until you are whole yourself. All those that come across your path are always a reflection of self. They are messengers to radiate back to you who you are in any given moment. You will always be surrounded by those that represent who you presently are, who you were in the recent past and who you are becoming in the near future, as you awaken to the true love of self.

Understanding the mirror those around you are reflecting back to you for your greater good and immediate benefit allows you to disengage yourself from another aspect of the lower mental mind known as judgment. If you are disturbed by someone, look upon them and see what is in within self that is so annoying because you choose not to be willing to see that the behavior of the individual is either something you are presently doing yourself, something you have done in the past, or something you are fearful of doing in the future.

Judgment also works the other way, when you find yourself enamored by someone, it is important for you to understand what you love about them is the same that is within you as well. You just don't see it as clearly when you are looking directly at yourself. When you release judgment of self in the understanding that you are your own true love, you can easily relinquish the debilitating judgment of others as well.

In order to fully realize your true love you must apply self -love; meaning do for self what you so willingly do for so many others. Give to self what you have been expecting or demanding others to give to you. Lovingly place yourself at the head of the line, rather in the rear where there is naught left for you. Place yourself not at the head of the banquet table, but rather in a seat at the round table of worthiness for all, as opposed to crawling at the feet of others scrounging for the leftovers or the crumbs that fall at their feet.

You are a queen or king, a Goddess or God because you are the personification of the love of the higher union that exists within you and you deserve the best of everything, not just the best of a few things or in some cases nothing good at all.

Use some of your money to purchase something for self, even if it is determined useless or frivolous by your logical mind or others. If you don't engage in the heart's desires, profound and or silly, you will surely have to spend the same amount of money or more on something else you were not expecting.

Or you may find yourself in a position to have to spend the same amount or more by surrendering it to a physician to help you heal the body that is reflecting back to you, via some disease or uncomfortable pain, your incorrect beliefs of not being love, loving, loved or lovable.

You may have become angry or resentful because you give and are not given to in return and thusly your body will abscess with poison that is being oppressed within and is seeking an avenue of outlet. Or your heart will be in pain and you will have what is called a heart attack; know the heart does not attack, it is reacting in defense of being ignored by you.

Apply self-love by living your life knowing its value and worth. Life is precious and precious few up until now have fully understood the gift of breath. Most of you allow others to live your life for you because you are in fear of loss of love, attention, safety or some other form of support.

The true love of you is independent and whole; it knows no lack and does not seek anything or anyone outside of self because it is always giving to self. It listens to the heart and follows the direction of what makes you happy. True love lives within a thriving joyful heart, not a fearful lacking mind.

Who cares if others call you a silly heart or a Pollyanna; remember misery loves, company because it lacks the courage to step out above or beyond the crowd or tribe. Misery is ego based, it will very boldly or subtly manipulate to get you to join it.

Your own inner true love is prepared to rescue the heart of you; it will whisk you away on a shining white horse of the spirit of courage. You can gain courage in being your own true love by going with what is right for you, rather than giving your power away to another out of fearful limiting incorrect belief of loss.

In divine support of the true love of self, you are being inspired to be willing to no longer dwell in the pain of the past, but to release the long held emotions that have been oppressed. Emotions are like water; they are energy in motion and if they are not honored, acknowledged and expressed in the moment of feeling them, they then stagnate and become a supportive pool for disease in the heart, mind and body.

There is no one denying you true love, other than you. No one is withholding the relationship you deserve, other than you.

Be yourself and trust your feelings, as they are navigating you to what is right for you so you do not compromise yourself for the false love and attention of another. Your emotions are a gift, they are the messengers within to help us become aware of what we are thinking about our self or any other situation for that matter. If we feel bad, we are having some fearful limited thought. If we feel good we are having an expanded loving thought.

Don't hide behind a smile, for if the feelings behind it are disingenuous, It is not OK to be grinning all the time. Emotions must be expressed; they must be given permission to be released in a healthy manner, regardless of whether they are good feelings or less than desirable feeling. You do this with integrity by honoring the feeling whatever it is in the moment you feel it. To dwell in them or project the responsibility of the feeling on to another is unhealthy, as either leads to more of the same vicious cycle of stuffing the emotion and then drawing an experience to you for which the emotion has a pathway to freedom.

This is the unconscious way and inevitably leads to more pain and frustration, more rejection and abandonment, as emotions also grow if they are contained. They become explosive like bombs because they are being resisted and what you resist will indeed persist and before long you explode in someone's face or you explode all over yourself and then the whole nasty business of believing you are not worthy of love begins again.

All of your life you have been trying to prove your worth by getting someone else to be your true love. There is nothing to prove because you already are the true love you are seeking. This would be humorous if it wasn't so sad and in time you will learn to also laugh about it.

The soul of you holds the mastery of the higher mind and lives in the presence of its own true love, it has no need to prove anything. It is the ego that demands acknowledgement. So in attempting to prove what already is known is a bit like banging your head against the wall and wondering why you are bleeding.

The union of the inner God, Goddess is the true loving relationship you.

They intend to be joined together, yet they need your cooperation to come within for your love rather than continually seeking it outside of yourself from another. Even though you ignore their desire they continuously send you unconditionally loving messages. Yet the ego of you would rather be right in its incorrect belief of being the lesser child of God/Goddess and therefore not deserving of love.

Your ego will crucifies you with its rightful indignations rather than be happy in the truth of being the magnificent child of God/Goddess. It would rather project blame onto another, than take responsibility in its fearful unwillingness to accept the truth and heal. It remains far too busy chasing after some man or woman refusing to be calm and listen to the true love that resides within.

If you want true love, than you focus all of your energy on the strength and courage to honor respect and love self. When we take the action to do this all others treat us with the same love, honor, respect and support.

It can be no other way, as no one can help but give to you what you are already giving to self. It works the opposite as well, if you give little or nothing to self than no others can give to you what you are unwilling to give to self.

Look at the real beauty you are, look beyond the physical into the eyes of true love. Gaze within the eyes of the soul you are and know your true love; this will restore your spirit and reawaken your passion

Your true love will compassionately listen to the victim of you, allowing it to be heard and also to shed its long held tears or anger.

This is when your need to look for love outside of yourself can end, as the victim has been heard and it will cease it's tight control over your life with its relentless insatiable needs and wants, as it will no longer fear giving and/or receiving love. It knows beyond the shadow of a doubt it is true love.

The victim is given its voice in a healthy, safe, loving environment where it is able to express all that it feels. The victim then becomes victorious; it wins and its life is filled with wows rather than being dogged by the woes.

In victory of choosing your value and worth, your aura will be crowned with the beauty, love and light of true love of self for all to see. You will know through the encounters with others, who or what each of them is to you and you will engage with them in the highest love, honor and respect of the true love of them as well.

Surround yourself in self loving images, dress yourself up in self loving apparatus and continue to look into the mirror directly into the eyes the windows of the soul and you will see your true love and when you are willing to see this clearly and live it each and every moment, that other if you still desire him or her, whom also knows and is practicing true love can stand with you and for you as an e qual life partner.

You will live in a relationship where there is no blame, no control or any other form of abuse. You will walk in heaven on earth hand in hand in love with self thereby having more than enough love to share with another.

Your heart will be ablaze with the passion for life, as opposed to an endless search for love. You will fully know the value of yourself and the gift you are.

Relationship Tips

Relationships exist between two people filled with emotions from their past experiences as well as their expectations for each other. This shows that relationships don't exist in a dead space or a vacuum. Since each person will be bringing their perspective to the relationship, it is expected that there could be some communication challenges. Luckily, communication is a skill that can be learned.

We're all pretty clear that talking is a form of communication, but if you only talk about everyday routine or superficial topics you're not really communicating. Intimacy and trust in a relationship are built on discussions of the things that really matter. This article is primarily about how to talk in a more open and rewarding manner with your significant other.

Communication is the lifeblood of your relationship; simply put, it can either make or break your romance. You can improve your relationship today, right now, by putting some of these tips for improving the communication in your relationship into practice.

❖ Listen.

This could be the most redundant tip that you've heard, but it warrants repeating. This part of communication is often taken for granted, because many of us are afraid of not being heard. This fear causes us to rush into speaking and forgetting about listening. When this happens, whether intentionally or not, both parties feel unheard and often misunderstood.

❖ Be open and honest with your partner.

To be in a real relationship, you must take a step toward opening yourself up to your partner. Though, some people have never been very open with others in their life, this is your chance to do so.

Honesty means that you don't hide your emotions, which could spawn little lies that will eventually turn out bigger ones. Not being honest is a barrier to effective communication. Being in a healthy nurturing relationship fosters openness between you and your partner.

Being open can include talking about your deep seeded thoughts and ideas which you may have never shared with anyone before. It means sharing your real self completely with your partner while accepting the possibility of disappointment and hurt. Yes, there is some risk involved, but the reward is far greater. You could be opening the door to the potential of unconditional love and acceptance.

❖ Pay attention to nonverbal signals.

Nonverbal communication is your body language, the tone of your voice - its inflection, eye contact, and physical contact. Learning to communicate better means that you need to learn how to read these signals as well as hear what the other person is really saying. Reading your partner's nonverbal signals takes time and patience, but the more you do it, the more attuned you will be to what they're really communicating. Here are some great examples:

• Folded arms in front of a person may mean they're feeling defensive or closed off.

• Lack of eye contact may mean they're not really interested in what you're saying, are ashamed of something, or find it difficult to talk about what's on their mind.

❖ A louder, more aggressive tone may mean the person is escalating the discussion and is becoming very emotionally involved. It might also suggest they feel like they're not being heard or understood.

Someone who's turned away from you when talking to you may mean disinterest or being closed off.

While you're reading your partner's nonverbal signals, be aware of your own. Make and maintain eye contact, keep a neutral body stance and tone to your voice, and sit next to the person when you're talking to them.

❖ Stay focused in the here and now.

Here and now means that the discussion, or an argument, should not be warped in another time. Keep the topic current since any topic from the past could most likely stir the conversation into something irrelevant. This could lead to more arguments.

❖ Try to minimize emotion when talking about important, big decisions.

Nobody can talk about important matters if they feel emotionally vulnerable or charged-up and angry. Those are not the times to talk about serious issues (like money, getting married, the kids, or retirement).

❖ Humor and playfulness usually help.

Being funny is not a requirement but a little sense of humor will do. Try to incorporate this sense of humor into most communication with your partner. This will help lighten up everyday frustrations. Playfulness reminds us that even if we have already grown up, there is always time to take a break from the seriousness.

Nobody is a perfect communicator all the time. But, improvement could be seen when you try any of these tips. They won't all work, nor will they work all the time. Better communication, however, start

with one person making the effort to improve, which often encourages the other to come along for the ride.

The Importance of Love Relationships for Your Mental Stability

Love relationships are very important in everyone's life. If you have traumatic love relationships when you are young, you'll face tragic future situations. If you have no love relationships at all, you'll develop a dangerous complex. You may even become mentally ill.

Love is in fact very dangerous. When you are in love, you cannot control your behavior. You cannot respect your moral principals. You become a slave of your feelings.

This is why the unconscious mind that produces your dreams sends you many dreams with objective information about the person you love.

You have many advantages in life when you are able to translate the meaning of dreams before getting married. The unconscious mind helps you find your perfect match, and have a perfect love relationship.

Wish I knew everything I know today when I was very young. However, at that time I was only gradually discovering the importance of the dream messages.

I had a warning about my husband in a dream before getting married, but I didn't believe that dreams should be trusted. I didn't know how to translate the meaning of dreams at that time. However, the warning was so clear that anyone could easily understand it.

This happened because dreams about love are not as symbolic as dreams about our mental health.

I should have listened to the voice that told me in a dream that my husband wouldn't love me for long. His love had a very short duration because he only wanted to take advantage of my naïve character. My husband was looking for a wife who would help him succeed in life. He never really loved me. He was an actor.

When I started having daily fights with him, I remembered the dream I had advising me that my husband's love would have a short duration. This fact helped me understand that I had to pay attention to dream warnings. My marriage was one of the worst mistakes I made in my life.

I didn't love my husband either. He was a very good friend who insisted very much on having a love relationship with me. In the end I decided to give him a chance.

This marriage couldn't have a happy end. It was based on mistakes and lies.

However, I couldn't understand this truth at that time. I was very ignorant, and I used to believe in unreal things. I was a slave of my rational psychological type. In other words, only my ideas were important for me. I belonged to the introverted psychological type based on thoughts. I had no feelings. I was totally insensitive.

My husband was a slave of his psychological type too. He belonged to the extroverted psychological type based on intuitions. He could guess the future development of reality, especially concerning business deals. He was always pursuing new money-making opportunities, but he didn't want to work too long on his plans.

Our personalities didn't fit together; we were totally different. However, we couldn't understand our own absurdity for deciding to get married. We thought we could shape our lives the way we wanted to.

There are many couples that make similar mistakes, for different reasons. There are people who are slaves of their feelings, and cannot logically understand that the person they love is not the ideal one for them. Other people care only about sexual pleasure, without paying attention to their inner feelings. I could give you numerous examples of love relationships based on false impressions and lies.

If you'll seriously think about all the mistakes you could make in life, you'll clearly understand that there are too many dangers threatening your happiness. A tragic love relationship can ruin your life and your mental stability forever.

You need protection.

I advise you to study the meaning of dreams about love because they are very simple, and this precious knowledge will save your life. Learn everything you can about the person you love before getting married. Learn also everything you can about yourself. You'll never find authentic happiness by chance.

I became a psychiatrist and psychologist for being able to help everyone find sound mental health by obeying the unconscious guidance in dreams. I'm only a human being, but the wise unconscious mind that produces our dreams has a divine origin.

The first ones I wanted to help when I started working online were the most desperate ones. I started helping people who wanted to commit suicide, especially young people who abuse their bodies. Self-abuse is one of the worst mental disorders existent today. It affects teenagers and young adults.

I had various conversations with teens who abuse their bodies. I also translated the dreams of a few of them.

They don't accept advice, and they don't want to follow psychotherapy.

I understood that I would only be able to help these teens by helping their parents. This is why I decide to work on helping everyone find love and happiness in life before getting married.

Everything begins with a marriage, this fatal step in everyone's life.

When the couple is not happy together, their children won't learn how to be happy, but develop mental illnesses and mental disorders. Everyone is very vulnerable to mental illnesses because we inherit a totally absurd primitive conscience into the biggest part of our brain.

I know that you don't want to think about depression now that you are young, and you have many beautiful plans. However, there are many hidden traps in your journey.

You can very easily lose your mental stability, form a problematic family, and then, have depressed children. Pay attention to this fact, and care about eliminating all the possibilities of failure from your destiny. You have this power if you obey the unconscious wisdom.

Don't make ridiculous mistakes for being a slave of your psychological type. Don't let your primitive conscience control your behavior. Find your perfect match before getting involved with the wrong person.

Relationship Advice- Problems Between Dating Couples

Relationship communication is a common problem among couples regardless of the status. Dating couples usually experienced a lot of relationship communication and relationship issues because the persons involve in the relationship do not want to listen. Most men I met want women to listen to them especially when they are talking about relationship issues. They only want the woman to make the adjustments. Then put a dot at the end of their sentence - That's IT!

This scene could be the worst nightmare of any woman. Communicating without really listening, for most part, in the side of the man, is very frustrating and irritating. This is especially true if you haven't settled the argument yet and he does not want to talk anymore. Relationship communication problems emerged from the unwillingness of men to settle relationship problems. They would just keep quite, prefer to talk with other topics, and the next thing you know, the problem recurs. Men hate drama, women hate drama too. The only big difference is that women prefer to talk and communicate any relationship issues before it worsen. Men prefer to be

46

silent and talk about relationship problems when it already is in its worst state.

If you talk about relationship problems, men should really sit in and talk to solve relationship issues. The best thing to make a woman stop talking about relationship problems is to really talk it out and settle whatever the problem between you and her is. I am not talking about making men crazy or driving them insane with a woman's blah blah. What I would like to emphasize in this discussion, is just to listen and communicate relationship issues. Relationship communication problem is very common among dating couples because most men usual behavior and reaction at the start of the discussion is to close their minds in such a way that they find it hard to even hear facts and see the discussion in the perspective of women.

How to Keep Your Woman Happy

47

A life's work is what you have taken on if you are to fully answer the question- how to keep your woman happy, but it is most definitely worth it. Once you have established your relationship and possibly even married the love of your life then you have to establish the solid framework for your relationship.

❖ Start with something simple like daily conversations, you may both have busy jobs or you may have a busy job while she has a busy home job looking after your children and the house, whatever you situation is talk to each other every day about anything NOT involving work, kids, home. In other words to each other about each other.

❖ Remember personal dates, anniversaries (obviously your wedding anniversary) but also, for extra points, remember the anniversary of your first meeting, or some other date that has meaning for just the two of you. If you have a memory like mine that forgets dates just set up a program on your computer or I phone, along with all your families' birthdays.

❖ Small gifts such as a small bunch of flowers, box of chocolates for no reason at all other than to show how much you care, maybe to say thank you for something she did or maybe simply if you had a good day at work and you want to share it with her.

❖ Romance was very important when you first met, now with all the pressures life is piling on the two of you it is even more important. Surprise her by arranging someone to look after the kids for a night and take her out, dinner, theatre, cinema wherever as long as it is a surprise and it is something she likes doing. Surprise and romance go hand in hand.

❖ Compliments are so easy to give I almost feel like I should not have to mention the subject. But lack of any compliments about anything she does well like a nice dinner, looking good, a new hairstyle, you make up the list will lead to trouble. Everybody likes to be appreciated.

❖ Respect is the other aspect of the giving compliments, you cannot give genuine compliments without establishing respect for your partner. You need to show respect in word and action.

❖ If your partner in a stay at home Mum then take some of the work form her shoulders, cook dinner one night, put the kids to bed anything to show her your care and appreciate the work she does for the family.

❖ The three most important words you must say to each other very day, preferably more than once, you will show each other every day in the things you do but to keep your woman happy just say "I love you"......

Keep working at it and you will find keeping your woman happy comes naturally.

HOW TO STOP A BREAK UP AND SAVE YOUR RELATIONSHIP

How to save your relationship is a very new mission for you. You have been dating long enough to know you are in love and you do not want to break up. The common phrase shoots through your mind..

"ALL IS FAIR IN LOVE AND WAR"

Meaning that almost ANYTHING GOES in these two arenas. It is a sad fact that many people will tell you is quite true after dating someone and being in a relationship for years only to be dealt a dear john letter (a break up or separation note from one lover to another)

Whatever Love Problem or Matter of The Heart You Have, the Answer is the SAME

51

Countless people are turning to Love Spells and Professional Spell casters to save their relationship and stop their break ups, divorces and separations. WHY? It is a Powerful and effective way to show your lover or ex lover just how much they mean to you. A Love Spell does NOT use evil, does NOT brain wash but rather uses natural energies to...

- ❖ SHOW YOUR EX JUST HOW MUCH YOU LOVE THEM
- ❖ ATTRACT THEM BACK INTO YOUR LIFE
- ❖ BLOACK ANY PROBLEMS OR FIGHTING THAT MAY HAVE CAUSED THE BREAK UP
- ❖ KEEP YOUR RELATIONSHIP STABLE AND HAPPY

You can safely, easily and quickly use Love Spells to stop your current break up, save your marriage, return an old lover and more. The limits are endless!

Relationship A dvice-Practical Tips For Handling Yourself When Upset

In our relationships there are always times when our partner says or does something that is upsetting. The instinctive response is to get angry and lash back. Most couples will say that communication problems is their number one concern in their marriage. At the same time each person wants to be heard and understood. Here are tips that will help you deal with your strong emotions.

A. When agitated first focus on gaining control over yourself.

Breathe deeply from your diaphragm. As you focus on your breathing you are getting control back over yourself. The goal is to be able to think about how you want to handle this situation. When one is all emotion it is impossible to think clearly. The emotional response then is reactive. Another tool is to count to 30 or 50. Counting is cognitive and gets you back to being able to think.

B. When you are able to think again you can figure out how you want to handle the situation

Once you have calmed yourself so you can think you can figure out what you want your partner to understand. Then talk about the issues in "I" messages instead of "you". You puts the other person on the defensive and they can no longer hear what you are saying. They are busy thinking of their rebuttal. The goal for you is to stay in your own head and be clear about what is going on with you.

C. Stay in the moment

Handle the situation at hand. If you bring in past hurts and frustrations it becomes too large to handle. By focusing on being clear as to why you got worked up in this situation you can work

for understanding and solutions.

Here is an example. Connie was furious with her husband when he took a call from his x-wife,who is the mother of his son, and continued talking with her after they had completed specific planning re: their son. Connie had felt for some time that his calls with her were too long and his tone was too nice. This time she tried to handle her feelings differently.

1. Instead of reacting immediately she breathed deeply many times

2. Then she counted to fifty

3. Now she was able to think (when one is all emotion it is impossible to think)

4. She decided that she did not want to talk with her husband at that time. In the past she had

expressed her anger at him immediately

5. Because she was still angry she realized she had to take care of her feelings

6. She went for a walk

7. While on the walk she decided that she would wait till they were both calm and then she

would speak in "I" messages to let him know what upset her and work with him

towards a solution to this recurring problem

8. When Connie got home she felt a lot better and she was pleased with the way she had

managed her feelings.

Learning to manage oneself is fundamental to healthy communication in relationships. In relationships one has to constantly think on two levels .

Relationship Advise - Tips to Effective Skills in Listening

Listening is one of the most important skills you can learn in life. Whether it is with your family, work or with your friends, listening is the key to find out and understand information you need to know.

There are different kinds and levels of conversation. There are conversations that are like ping pong, a natural back and forth exchange. Some are light and some more in depth interactions.

These tips will facilitate a more meaningful conversation as well as show respect to someone who wants to share something significant with you. These skills will work in casual situations with family and friends or more formal situations at work.

1. Allow the person to fully express themselves and their feelings without interrupting. This takes responsibility on

our part and humility. We humble ourselves when we set aside our own desire to be heard and listen to someone else. The interesting thing is when you are willing to listen to someone else, they usually return the favor and show interest in listening to you as well.

2. Be present with them. If you are in person, look them in the eye.

When you walk or eat together or on the phone and it would be awkward for continual eye contact, make sure you simply let them know you are with them. Let it come natural but be present.

3. Listen to your heart, not just your mind. Get a feeling of empathy for what they experienced or felt.

When you develop listening skills, you will have power in your relationships. There are many more tips to effective listening and ways to work though conflict and have peace in your relationships.

Relationship Advise-The Top Hurdles and How to Overcome Them

In today's society, fast track living is the norm. We may go from work, to the gym, to picking up kids (if you have kids). to coming home and making dinner, and then sleep only to wake up and do it all again the next day. With our lives being so busy we may wonder where we can find time to work on our relationships!

The truth is, although life can get hectic at times, building on our relationships with solid effective communication strategies are what brings us together and keeps us together regardless of the everyday situations we're faced with. It's important to understand the common communication mistakes couples often make in order to work out effective strategies to understand one another and work together as a team long term.

Communication Mistake #1 -- Negativity and Escalation

The most common communication mistake couples often make involve negativity and escalation. The occurs when partners respond to one another negatively, with each response getting worse and worse until finally one person oversteps the boundaries and makes a hurtful statement.

How to change this: if you're in a relationship you most likely know intimate details about one another. This includes information that could be hurtful should you use it in a condescending way. When you find yourself in an argument with your partner recognize your feelings and notice when you feel yourself getting so heated you may bring up a sensitive topic. In other words, step back from the situation before making hurtful statements that could escalate a simple topic into an outright war.

Communication Mistake #2 -- Invalidation

Feeling comfortable enough to express your fears and worries should be welcomed in a relationship. But partners can sometimes take this for granted and don't try to see where the other is coming from. This includes putting down the other person's thoughts and feelings. For example, your partner may be having a hard time at work with his boss. Instead of comforting and listening you may think he's overreacting and tell him so. This is a communication mistake as you're invalidating your partner's feelings.

How to change this: take the time to listen to your partner. If he or she has a concern, hear it out and offer advice only when asked.

Communication Mistake -- Avoidance and Withdrawal

When one partner avoids confrontation, the other may feel the need to pursue and press a subject further. An avoidance of a subject therefore turns into a game of tug of war, sending the avoider further away and the pursuer more forceful in getting the other to talk. Even if the pursuer has good intentions, this doesn't solve the problem at hand. Instead it makes the problem even worse!

How to change this: the way you start a discussion will affect how the other person responds. If you are the pursuer and your partner tends to avoid, approach subjects with a positive, caring opening statement instead of a negative statement.

RELATIONSHIP INVESTMENT

I love to chuckle at all the spam headlines from the financial industry. They promise fortunes to the unwary. So, today's headline is a bit tongue in cheek. However, not entirely so.

I see so many people taking their relationships for granted, investing little or nothing in them, and then being surprised when they get a dismal return. But, it really doesn't take all that much effort to make them much better, with just a little more effort to make them much, much better.

What about you? Will you invest heavily in your relationship this year?

Pay Yourself First

The financial budgeting industry uses this phrase a lot. By paying yourself first, they mean putting money aside for savings and retirement before you pay any bills, before you spend on anything else, and before you fritter it away in all the other ways possible.

This works for your relationship, as well. Pay yourself first. Put your relationship first. Put weekly dates on your calendar before anything else. Budget relationship money before anything else. Be intensional about those sweet, little thank you gifts you're going to give throughout the year.

The first thing Pam and I do every morning is snuggle and cuddle for a half hour to an hour after the alarm goes off. What a great way to start the day! Pay yourself first!

Are You A Buyer, or A Looker?

Classical marketing teaches a very clear dictum: A buyer is a buyer, and a looker is a looker. Marketers are supposed to spend all their time on true buyers, and forget about engaging the lookers, because lookers just aren't serious about doing or buying much of anything.

When it comes to your relationship, are you a buyer?

Will you invest the time, attention, energy, and money required to move things to the next level or above?

Time: Find those few moments everyday. Have a date every week. Create a special weekend every month. And remember those birthdays and anniversaries!

Attention: Really attend to your partner. Listen, and really hear!

Energy: Save some energy for the relationship. Figure out how to not use it all up on the job, or the kids, or on your hobby. Energize your relationship!

Money: Buy books and tapes, and read them and listen to them! Invest in a marriage counselor for a quarterly check up on your relationship portfolio.

And the Best Investment of All

Face into your anxiety. Emotional Intimacy means becoming closer to another human being than you ever thought possible. It's probably closer than you've ever been comfortable with before. That means being afraid to some extent. It means tolerating the fear and talking about things you never thought you could. Your ability to do so will grow with your relationship and you'll be amazed with how wonderfully close you've become.

Relationship Advce-Three Steps When Relationship Get Crazy

Even good relationships can get crazy and spiral out-of-control when emotions, deep vulnerability and egos take hold. This is when love, logic and clear thinking goes out the window and you are at a total loss for what to do. Continuing to communicate in this state of craziness is a fruitless and frustrating exercise.

Deanna and I are the developers of neuroscience systems for establishing rapport, understanding and harmony. These tools are utterly useless when emotions run rampant. They work best when both parties are in calm and receptive states-of-mind to use them.

As a married couple and business partners, we have learned that these strategies work well when things get crazy. Perhaps what we do will help you when communications get out of hand with significant people in your life.

1. Say you're sorry. Admit you played a role in the situation. Say you will learn from it and try to avoid this happening again. Even if one of you says this with authenticity, the statement opens the door for a discussion.

2. Agree you want to heal the relationship. This is the defining moment that establishes the intention and commitment to work on the relationship. Both parties saying this with sincerity is ideal. Agreeing you want to heal the relationship and saying "you're sorry" can be done in person, text, voice mail, email or a thoughtful card.

3. Revisit the situation when cool heads prevail. Time apart should be spent thinking about your role in the problem and identifying the "hot buttons" that ignited the chain reaction. Begin by saying, again, that you are sorry

and want the relationship to be better and stronger. Avoid the dead-end street of defending your position and attacking the other person. Neither is right or wrong. Remember that both of you are doing the best you can at every moment. The mood you are in, "hot buttons," incomplete information and jumping to conclusions are more than enough to set off a chain reaction of craziness in any relationship. Share with one another the lessons learned. Convey your ideas to improve the relationship. Focus on positive things you both can do in the future to better communicate with one another.

These three steps will help you get your relationships back on track when rational behavior leaves the scene. This method has worked well for us. The steps are grounded in practical and safe neuroscience principles. They demonstrate positive and caring behaviors important for healthy relationships. Give it a try the next time things get crazy.

How To Beat Depression With The Strength of Your Relationship

Your partner while under the influence of these depressed feelings seems, to you, to be unable to appreciate the better things in life that you are trying to provide. They behave in an illogical way and you are tempted to feel that your efforts are wasted, but this is not true. Because you are with them they feel as though they can cope better although they may not be capable at this stage of communicating that to you.

The fact that you have remained with them, means more than you will ever know, though because of their condition they may try to force you to leave them, this is difficult for you to deal with as it may be the exact opposite of what they really want and need.

I you decide to stay then you would be best advised to found out as much as you can about your partners mental condition. By gaining an understanding of what it is you may be able to work out what brought these terrible feelings on. The fear of perceived failure is a common cause most often happening when they loose a job or something happens that they feel was not their fault and so they should not be in this situation, feeling that it is unfair that they should be here. Whatever started this depressive state it can quickly escalate even if the relationship between you is strong.

If you are not careful taking care of someone with these depressed moods can spread to you, the fact that you have learned as much as you can about your partners condition should make it easier for you to be aware of your own state of mind.

If your partner's condition seems to be deepening or if you find that you are both starting to show symptoms of the condition then seek help form a psychologist or counselor, professional help is often essential to break the hold of this condition. The depression will be helped by your constant attention but this can be very warring on you, if this is the case then try to step back and take a break to renew you energy to go on.

Sometimes the cause of the condition can be historic in that your partner could have had a bad breakup in the past which they have never fully recovered from, they may live with irrational fear that this will happen all over again with your relationship, even though it may be a strong secure relationship. Seek help from a relationship counselor as often the strain brought about in one partner by the depression of the other means that without help the relationship will break, counseling will restore the balance.

A possible sweet solution - scientific studies that dark chocolate eaten in moderation has a multitude of health benefits not only for the heart but also for the brain as it contains theobromine, caffeine and other stimulants and help with a feeling of wellbeing, but more importantly recent research has revealed that the presence of serotonin in dark chocolate acts as an anti-depressant.

Never give up where there is love there is hope, just have faith in the help you are giving and that it will allow you to overcome this condition. Seek professional help as early and as often as you can, faith and love will show you the way to beating depression with a strong relationship.

How To Avoid Marriage Breakup Over Financial Stress

Are you having relationship or marriage issues and one of the main causes is Finances? Well, you are not alone. In fact, financial stress is one of the biggest reasons for divorce. Financial stress and struggles can cause the best of relationships to breakup. Knowing how to get past it can save your relationship, and bring you closer together.

We are all feeling the pain of the lack of financial security, and have been for a few years now. Jobs have been lost, retirement funds are gone, along with savings accounts. You may have already lost your home, or are about to, because those great jobs are not being replaced. You don't mean to blame each other, it wasn't their fault, but, deep down the resentment starts to build.

Regardless of the lifestyle you once had, the one thing you need to keep in mind, is why you got together to begin with. If you and your partner have been together for a long time, or even married for many years, you have to remember that, at some point, you may have struggled before. I can not sit here and tell you that "love conquers all." But, I can tell you, that surviving hard times can absolutely make your relationship stronger and make you a better team.

Part of this is learning how to work together. No one person should be responsible for figuring out the solutions by themselves. "Better or worse", remember? Well, here you are. Sit down together and openly discuss your situation, and your bills. Separate the must haves from the we can do without for now. You will be surprised by the compromises you can make. As you start more open discussions, you will also be surprised by the ideas you can come up with for cutting corners.

Go grocery shopping together. That way you are both involved in choosing less expensive meals, and you can actually enjoy picking out new ideas and combinations for healthy, inexpensive, and creative meals. This way, you also won't have one person saying "why are we eating this", and the shopper having to justify the budget continuously and feeling defensive about the choices they make.

Renting a movie, or finding something you both want to watch on TV are also a plus, with an inexpensive bottle of wine and some popcorn. Play video games? Your kids would enjoy you joining them for an evening with your thumbs! Instead of going out, go for walks together in the evenings. Not only is it good exercise, but it allows you to have conversations you would not normally have time for. Another little thing no one really thinks about is, save your change in a bowl or jar. That way, if something comes up that you would really like to do, go cash it in and do it! Those change jars come in handy for treat night.

The key thing here is talk to each other. You are in this together, so decide how you are going to survive this bump in the road together. Everyone may have to give up a little something here, and a little something there, but, if everyone gives up something, for the good of the cause, you will feel better about your situation, and each other.

Relationship Advice -How To Attract A Man

Trust me, we (women) have all been there. Whether you are single or divorced, the situation seems to repeat itself over and over again. We make a lot of mistakes along the way. We feel our "picker" is broken and may even give up for a while. I can tell you that after years of trying to figure out my own broken "picker" as well as spending years watching other women go through the same thing, it became unanimous that there were just no good men left! That's actually not the case. There are plenty of good men out there who are looking for the "right" woman to have Love and a Long Lasting Relationship.

Now, don't get me wrong here, I spent years blaming myself as is in the nature of women as a rule. Not because we are at fault, but because someone has to take the blame because that keeps order in our lives, and we, as women, like order in our lives. If we were in a relationship with an alcoholic and got burned, the next man we go out with who has a beer doesn't have a prayer. If we had a relationship with someone who was a workaholic and the next guy has to work on a Saturday night, he doesn't have a prayer. Then we blame ourselves for not giving them a chance. Closure.

There are many reasons why women have relationship challenges. Believe it or not, the main reason is that women simply don't understand men. You see, we think men think like women and that is simply not true. Men are not nearly that complicated. Our thought processes are not even close when it comes to relationships. As women, we think we know what we want in a man. Men actually don't have a clue until it's right in front of them.

You see, we talk to our girlfriends, sisters, and mothers, about our relationship issues. That's not a bad thing because it gives us a chance to unload and actually creates closer relationships...with them. We ask them for advise and they give their opinions freely. We are usually willing to take that advise because, well, why not? I will tell you why not. Because they are not in your relationship with your guy. They may be divorced (so that didn't work) or they are in the same situation you are in. Great friends, lousy counselors. Now, I'm not saying all their advise is bad or even wrong! But, the wrong advise can make your situation worse or blow your chance of a relationship all together. Many women turn to popular women's magazines for advise, WRONG, WRONG, WRONG! This advise is given by women as well and don't give women any insight to understanding men at all.

Understanding men is actually quite simple. They want to be finessed, bewitched, and seduced by a woman. A man will gladly give anything to the woman who makes him FEEL GOOD. I don't mean a few sexual tricks in the bedroom or cooking great meals. Although these things are certainly appreciated, there is so much more to it than that. Do you know what the #1 "man repellant" is? Or, the main reason why men get married and stay married? Do you know the "Kiss of Death" in a relationship and how to avoid it? Did you know that your defenses build a very detectable wall without you even knowing it?

These are all very important things to know, and there's more. The best part is, you don't have to give up who you are to get the man you want. Men really do want you to be yourself. The truth is, we don't have to look like Jennifer Lopez. That's not really what they are looking for. "The Woman Men Adore...And Never Want To Leave" can give you the valuable information you need to attract and keep any man. It works! You can actually get your man to give you the world just by knowing what he really wants.

Relationship Advice

Relationship Advice- Remaining in the Place of Love

As the years go by in a long term relationship, it can be difficult to communicate as if your in love. I know you are still in love but the ego, always wanting to be heard, can easily rear it's ugly head and make it so hard to be centered. Communication on a balanced level is one of the most important factors in keeping a relationship long term. It's all too simple to get caught up in your world...one where it seems as if everything is going wrong and no one understands. Maybe your significant other doesn't fully understand, but expressing your ability to let them in and keep them in creates bonding.

When typical fights break out what do you really hear? It's not just complaints about who left the toilet seat down, dirty socks left around the house or who didn't take out the garbage. What you will hear behind those words is a cry for attention. "Listen to me...I still matter. I'm still me." When you realize the intention of most relationship arguments, it's easy to take a step back and include your lover in your communication. In a long term relationship, you can lose your identity very quickly. When both lovers say "I hear you" the balance of communication takes place.

Most relationship articles will tell you that listening is the most important part of communication. But beyond just listening, an acknowledgment has to take place. The person you love so dear is crying for attention, not just from you...remember you are the one who pays the most attention to her, but from the world. Bonding the strength of a long term commitment means to create a team. One that sets you apart from the rest of the world. One that tells your lover that you are not only "there for them," but there for each other. We need to know that are partner has our back, understands the things we feel and knows wholeheartedly that we are an inseparable team.

It's easy to get up in the little things. Seeing the big picture takes a little more discipline. But the payoff is huge! Can you hear the words of your partner and what they are really saying? Of course you can...that's why you love them.

How to Stop Hurting Yourself and Your Relationships by Over Giving in 7 Simple Steps

Are you damaging your relationships by over giving? Are you a giver who often ends up feeling taken advantage of over and over again by takers?

The arch nemesis of healthy balanced relationships is over -giving and unfortunately many of us do it all the time. Often girls especially are socialized to give and give and learn to feel satisfaction not from the reciprocation but from the giving process "It feels so good to know I am helping someone else". While I am not saying it's bad to help someone who needs it or to participate in charity work, you much make sure you are not over giving in your personal relationships to the point where you are creating an out of balance relationship with someone.

This is what I see a lot-especially from female clients "I just give and give to my family and they just don't appreciate it" or "In my relationship with my partner it feels like I do all the work" or "my ___ (brother, sister, son...) has so many problems and I help them but it doesn't get any better" OR what I think it is the most destructive of all "My boyfriend has so many problems, I am helping him work them out then he will be happy and we will have a great relationship".

The thing is we do this because we are getting something out of it. In romantic relationships we think if we "fix" them they will be so grateful they will love us forever. Sorry guys but that never happens. I can tell you from both personal and professional experience that IF the person (who by the way may not actually want to get better) with your help were actually able to solve all their problems most likely they would not turn around and thank you for your help, they would most likely move on after they had healed leaving you feeling drained and used.

I have seen it so many times with woman and men who have helped people through both physical and emotional challenges only to see that person break up with them and marry the next person they meet leaving the giver feeling devastated and not knowing what happened.

It goes both ways too because often "givers" are not even open to receive. I know for myself I recently had a friend who was always giving me advise and help yet every time I tried to reciprocate she wouldn't let me. I felt like she was getting resentful at our one sided friendship but even though I could see what was going on I couldn't seem to do anything about it.

No healthy person wants a relationship that is not reciprocal but plenty of unhealthy people want that which is why givers so often get taken advantage of.

So how can you tell if you are over giving? Look for these signs.

- ❖ -Do you send twice as many emails as you receive?
- ❖ -Do you feel drained after the interactions with this person or persons?
- ❖ -Are you expecting something from the other person that you don't seem to be receiving?
- ❖ -Are you feeling taken advantage of or used (if you are feeling it, you probably are)

Now it's easy to blame the receiver but it's not entirely their fault. You set this up yourself by either not setting proper boundaries, over giving from the beginning and/or not being open to receive when the other person tries to reciprocate. Trust me people will only try to give to you so many times before they give up and let you keep giving without receiving anything.

The other part of this is that there are plenty of people out there who just love givers because they get to take, take, take and not have to give back. Those are all the ex-s you dumped (hopping you didn't marry them first) because they never appreciated you.

So how do we fix this?

Oh boy that is a loaded question because the reality is even if the relationship or connection is worth saving it's not easy for either you or the other person to change that dynamic, but it can be done and here's a few things that can help.

1) BACK OFF-Backing off means giving space for people to give to you and if they don't eventually invite you to coffee or ask how you are doing this may not be a connection worth saving.

2) Don't give advise unless specifically asked for, give support. My friend Jackleen who is a professional coach is the best at this If I email her and complain about a problem I am having she says something like.."That's rough, we all go through that sometimes" Basically she gives me support not advise unless I schedule an appointment,

then I get advice. An over giver friend emails me a 2 page list of how I should fix it. Appreciated but not exactly what I wanted since she never asks me for advice. Most people prefer support unless you specifically ask for advice.

3) You don't have to share everything: it's OK for some cool treasures or great things you discovered to be just yours. Often we unconsciously give to others what we hope to get ourselves thinking we have "to give to get". Next time you feel compelled to give to someone, cut out the middle man and give it to yourself.

4) Ask for something: even if you don't really need it, this can help bring the give and take into a connection and start the ball rolling.

5) Say no sometimes: Practice this "Sorry but I can't babysit your kids on Thursday" "Sorry, I know you are in a tough spot but I really don't have any extra money right now" even if you don't need to, give yourself permission to say "no" just because, its good practice for when you

have to say no for a good reason.

6) Find ways of getting more fulfillment: I am a recovering severe over giver so I understand this problem well. When I got a job working in a hospital I started getting paid for what I gave and I received great satisfaction from this. The result was I stopped over giving in my personal life since that need was being met in a more healthy way. Find a healthy way of getting that need for satisfaction met in a way that allows you to keep healthy personal relationships.

7) Work on your receiving skills: Like I said most over givers are very bad receivers and you have to change that in order to create balance. Watch your receiver friends and see what they do. They tend to accept things that are offered to them even if it's not an immediate need, they ask for what they want/need and most importantly they feel they deserve the good things they get and SO DO YOU, so practice being more like them.

Relationship Advice

Relationship Communication Problems

The theory is simple! Intelligent, effective communication is vital if you want your relationship to survive. Everything in the relationship revolves around communication, after all, how are you going to know such basics as what your partner wants and needs from the relationship, how will you be able to plan for the future. Like all great theories, putting into practice can be a whole lot harder and more complicated than it at first looks. Male and female relationship communication problems begin at quite a basic level, we communicate differently.

As equal partners in a relationship you both have an equal responsibility for making the relationship work. If you want to help your partner get what they need from the relationship and help them grow then you need to know everything about them. You need to be able to get under their skin to find out what makes them tick, and that means entering areas in which they are vulnerable. Unfortunately not everyone is comfortable about talking about their feelings and emotions, people can get uncomfortable about making themselves vulnerable. If you will not let your partner in then how can they support you, without an environment of mutual support how can you build a trusting relationship, and a relationship is built upon trust.

There are the unfortunate differences in how men and women communicate. Women are more likely to ask for help, whereas society has conditioned men to be strong and handle all their problems by themselves. Trying to hide things, cover things up or pretend that something is not happening is not healthy for the relationship. When you keep secrets you are putting up walls between you and your partner, in effect pushing them away from you. No matter how many times you tell your partner that there is no problem, your body language will betray you and you will look as if you are hiding something. If your partner thinks that you are hiding something then their trust in you will start to waver and suspicion will grow. Relationship communication problems are always best dealt with by being totally open and honest.

When you are talking with each other you need to focus on your partner, let them say what they have to say and listen to what they have to say. It is not always easy to listen properly because your mind is automatically running over what your response will be. You might not be to clear on some of the things that your partner is saying so clarify by saying something along the lines of, "so what you are saying is...", it shows that you are taking notice and that you actually care about your partner.

Wether you like it or not you will have arguments or differences of opinion, they might not be pleasant but at least they can highlight issues that need dealing with. It is far to easy to easy to shout and scream at each other, which might give a few seconds satisfaction but achieves, nothing. One or both of you might have egos that need to win every argument, hurrah for your egos but please remember that in a relationship conflict, no one wins. This may come as a surprise to some of you, but it is not a sign of weakness to let your partner say their piece, it is a sign of respect and strength.

To effectively deal with relationship communication problems you need to be able to compromise. This is not some silly little point scoring game, you are not out for what is best just for your, you have to work for what is best for the relationship. Both of you need to deal with your issues rationally and calmly. You focus on each issue one at a time and come up with a solution together, one which you are both happy with.

Be aware of your body language. You can say one thing but there is every chance that if it is not the truth then your body language will give you away, so be honest as body language cannot mask emotions. Your partners body language is also a great way to judge your partners mood and how they are feeling, you might be able to show how much you care by responding to a need that you partner has not had to mention.

Relationship communication problems can be dealt with by communicating intelligently. You could be together for decades so learn how the other thinks and feels. As time passes you will change, your partner will change and as you both change then so will your wants, needs and your relationship. Be ready for those changes and adapt to them as they occur. Let your partner know that you love them, appreciate them and care for them, and do it on a regular basis. Do not forget that communication is a two way process, the person speaking has to get their message across to your partner he needs to listen to everything. It will take some work on the part of both of you, but it will be worth it.

Being a student of life I thought it about time to get my ideas down in the hope that they will help people with whatever difficulties they are facing. If you want to read further help and guidance in dealing with relationship problems then my site might be able to help.

Relationship Communication Problems, the Crisis in Male-Female Conversation Crying Out For Attention

Relationship communication problems are very common relationship problems. There are a number of ways we can look at what these basic relationship problems are all about.

One of the first things to say is it seems men are primarily responsible for the issues associated with marital and relationship problems to do with communication.

I imagine a lot of men reading the last sentence would become very defensive about that statement and think it is another example of male bashing.

On the other hand there is every chance many women reading it would identify with what is said and wholeheartedly agree with the statement.

Adele Horin, a columnist in the Sydney Morning Herald, writes about relationship communication problems. She says there is a "..shortage of men that women can relate to. The crisis in male-female conversation cries out for more attention. Relationships are being destroyed, or aborted at first date..."

She goes on "Say a woman has found a man... Before long she has detected the fatal flaw. 'He just doesn't listen. He won't talk to me.' She thinks it is an individual problem, and that a more sympathetic conversational mate can be found..But this conversational crisis is bigger than any individual. It is gender-wide. And it starts young."

Boys imitate the modeling of other men and she says, "..boys - with exceptions of course - soon develop the minimalist style mothers, girlfriends and wives despair of."

A male reader responded to Adele's column in the letters page of the "Herald". He wrote, "..The fact is women are terrible communicators."

He added, "Women arrogantly take the stance that their way is superior, against all the evidence, and refuse to be rational, constructive and inclusive. Instead of trying to change male behavior to suit themselves - a tactic that seems to be failing - perhaps it would be better to accept their own shortcomings and work on modifying them."

Can you imagine the relationship communication problems experienced with someone like this man. I think he is so extreme and when I first read it I thought he might have been saying all this with his tongue in his cheek, but I don't think so. I think he is serious.

Horin asks the question about how men are like this when she says, "Who knows how these patterns are established?"

I've got some idea about how this has all come about and I intend to go ahead and explain this and at the same time show how this has created relationship communication problems.

There has been a widespread belief in the world that men are superior to women. This was the accepted view for thousands of years. Some think this is no longer the case, yet there is ample evidence to suggest it is still firmly in place.

It is not my intention to expand on this here, but simply to state it as a fact. I am now going to show how this has impacted males to bring about the conversational crisis.

If, as males, we see ourselves as superior, this places us on a higher level and women on a lower level. On the whole, men seem unable to feel equal to women: they must be superior or they are inferior.

It's like a competition, it is win/lose. If I'm not in charge or on a higher level, then she will be, and I'll be on a lower level and she'll be in charge, and it's not supposed to be like that.

So when it comes to relationship communication problems, it is paramount men demonstrate how the proper structure is in place. What better way of doing this than not listening or taking any notice of women.

It is like men might as well be saying, "who do you think you are, you are not on my level, I don't have to listen to you, or acknowledge you. You don't count anyway, so what you have to say is not important."

When we listen to others, we are acknowledging they are on the same level, and are equally important to us.

Other aspects of this are, when it comes to feelings, if we see ourselves as being superior, it follows we are above all that. It's okay for you inferior lot to get caught up in that rubbish, as that is the stuff of weaklings, but we are not like that.

The other matter related to this that creates relationship communication problems, is the issue of the ability to understand and share the feelings of another - in other words empathy.

Men are notorious for their lack of empathy. It is just like the listening question. Given women are inferior and therefore don't count, why should men be concerned about how they feel, because women don't matter.

This is the only way I have been able to make sense of these relationship communication problems. I'm sure many women can identify with my explanation, and I hope I have given men some things to think about, and how they can make changes.

Relationship Advice - How to Talk Better With Your Partner

Relationship communication problems occur because each and every one of us is a unique individual. We may have some similarities in hairstyle, tastes, attitudes, etc, but nobody has all the same aspects we do. Thus, when we communicate with each other, it is not surprising to find that we can have problems. Each of us think differently, has different perspectives, beliefs and opinions. It is through the understanding of the people around you, the people in your relationship, that you can learn to accept the differences we all have.

Many recommend being honest with your partner and sharing your thoughts and opinions openly. That is actually a good action to take since magicians, psychics and mind readers are the stuffs of legends. However, do be careful with the way you use your words. You may be stating a simple truth, which is that your partner is not doing something right, but from your partner's sensitive point of view, you may appear to be criticising and condemning. Knowing how to use the right words, perhaps at the right time as well, could help prevent a misunderstanding. Even the most patient and calm-tempered person would have a weak point which you may accidentally hit and get them enraged.

When saying your piece, think first before speaking. Think about what you are going to say and avoid making any criticising statements. Your main purpose is to send your partner a message about what is happening in your relationship. Slowly add the idea of what you feel about the situation. Do not make any statements that involve your partner. This, always remember to keep your feelings under control and remain composed. You would want to avoid sounding accusatory and making your partner defensive, which may become a barrier to your communication.

Avoiding the blame would be best to start a discussion about a possibly sensitive issue. Convincing your partner that he will not be criticised or that is it all right for everybody to make mistakes would open his mind and allow him to reflect on his mistakes and reconsider his actions. Making him guilty or criticising him will only upset him, resulting in undesirable consequences.

Here is an example of how a person could phrase it if a wife is too caught up in her shopping spree: "Shopping is a great way to distress and is much fun to have new items in our possession, particularly since you have worked so hard to keep our house in shape. Thank you, but I do hope we will have enough savings for rainy days. As we all know, earning money isn't easy." Note that the main issue is not addressed directly and instead, it praises the wife for her hard work as part of the family, thus making it sound as if her shopping extravaganzas are deserved.

The last sentence will send to her the message that she needs to watch how she spends the money and when she thinks of the reason herself, she convinces herself.

It may be difficult for us to change the way we speak, and maybe even harder to maintain our changed speeches, but if we keep trying and practising, we would eventually learn to say the right things at the right time, and with ease.

Relationship Advice -Reasons Why Women Leave Relationships

For many men it might be really daunting understanding why a woman would leave a relationship. Once in a while a woman may leave a man for no apparent reason but really it is rare that a woman would leave a relationship without a pretty serious reason for doing so.

A woman may leave a man for various reasons but below we are going to talk a little bit more on two of the leading reasons that majorly account for why women leave relationships and these are the issues of neglect or abandonment and lack of emotional satisfaction.

Neglect or Abandonment

Women often complain that the men in their lives just stop being the active participant they used to be in the relationship and tend to pay more attention to things that most women contend are just trivial compared to the roles they play in the relationship.

When a woman starts feeling that her spouse has started taking her for granted in no small ways and no longer pays her attention or care about her opinion on issues concerning the relationship, she starts pondering on why she is hanging on to it. When a man stops doing the things he used to do for his woman without any justifiable reasons given to her for his actions, this create a serious problem for the woman and her mind at this point might have already left the relationship.

Most time after too much of neglect, most women just hang around hoping that she might get his attention, make him listen to her and probably have a change of heart in the way he treats her. However, this is not always the case, as most men never realises this neglect and simply just demises her intention.

Therefore neglect can be statistically said to accounts for almost all of the reasons why women leave relationships and therefore it goes saying that women leave men when they are neglected.

❖ **Lack of Emotional Satisfaction**

Due to the way nature has wired women differently from men, they think and reason a bit differently. Testosterone which is the dominant hormone makes the men to act and think masculine making them aggressive and sexually stimulated by sight. The women's dominant hormone estrogens makes them rather act like females they are causing them to want attention, kind gestures, affection nice words, compliments and things like flowers. These differences in hormonal makeup make the men to be cold and calculative while the women tend to be warm and emotional.

The lack of understanding of this natural phenomenon can cause a lot of rancour in a relationship. Men often think that when a woman is involved with them sexually that the woman is emotionally in tuned to them. This is not always so as it is not the sex that makes the relationship great for her even though it plays a part in it, it is having her general emotional needs satisfied that is paramount.

The need for communication in a relationship is the most important emotional need a woman needs to be fulfilled in a relationship. She needs the man to wholeheartedly listen to her, value her input in discussions.

Also men who consider their partner's feelings and opinions during decision making create an atmosphere for understanding, emotional bonding, intimacy and romantic love and thus they can effectively fulfil their partner's emotional needs.

❖ Having Great but Unrealistic Expectation

No matter how ironic you may think it is, a lot women still dream of their "Knight in shining armour" and the "happy-ever-after" when it comes to relationship. They still dream of these fairy tale expectations in their relationships.

When a woman with these ideals that are nowhere close to real life demands them from her man, there would definitely be problems in that relationship and most of them might be impossible for the man to live up to. The best the man can do in a situation like this is to try and understands what exactly her expectations are and try compromising in try to satisfy her.

❖ Pressure from friends and relatives

Although this might sound a little trivial, it is a fact that a lot of women without personal conviction about their place in a relationship may easily succumb to pressure from their peers or family members. However unfair it might seem, this is often the case when she cannot make her friends or family members to like her spouse. Except her love is strong willed and she is deeply attracted to the man, the manipulation of her peer group and family may become unbearable for her and thus she might leave the relationship.

❖ Lack of Attraction

To be just here, just as men would contemplate leaving a relationship where the attraction between partners no longer exists, a woman might likely be tempted to leave a relationship that has become more a chore than fun.

A man that is all out to please his woman without adding any form spontaneity to it risk losing the attraction her holds for his woman since these acts some become mundane and uninteresting. A man should seek ways to bring variety into the relationship and have a sense of confidence, direction and strength to lead the relationship in the right direction.

The Most Critical Skill For A Successful Relationship

The most critical relationship skill you have is your ability to communicate. Research has shown that poor communication in a relationship is a key factor in the failure of that relationship. It is also found that the happiest married couples are the best at communication. Good communication increases marriage satisfaction more than any other factor.

How you talk to your mate will determine how happy they are in the relationship. Talking to your spouse is not about just a monologue, it includes listening. Spouses who feel understood by their partners will have a much easier time expressing their true feelings. Good communication req uires active listening, which means you must be able to repeat back to your spouse what was said in your own words and get agreement.

When we talk about communication, it is more than just talking. It is actually much more complex than that. There are people who get entire graduate degrees studying communication. Communication is the entire process of imparting, or making known, a meaning of some kind to the other person. We primarily focus on using language to do that, however, the way we say it and the non-verbal cues contribute to the meaning of the words significantly. It is the meaning behind what is said that really counts. If your spouse says to you, "I can't believe you bought me such a nice gift", did the way they say it sound like a child's squeal of delight, or like a wife's angry message to her husband?

You also can communicate a lot with silence. Giving someone the silent treatment can be interpreted as a punishment, and an act of anger. Not answering a question, or simply not speaking in a social situation where speaking is usually expected can communicate a meaning to the other person. Sometimes silence can be awkward and communicate a state of discomfort or disconnection. Whether you like it or not, you are always communicating. These days even the time it takes you to respond to an email or a text can communicate something. Do you respond immediately, or does it take you a day or so?

In any case, communication is a key when it comes to building intimacy. We must be able to share our thoughts and feelings effectively. As you grow closer, good communication becomes even more critical. When you get serious with someone in a romantic relationship, there is an increased expectation that this person would have greater interest in what you say and speak to you with greater sensitivity than other people. The outcome of discussions you have with your partner will largely be determined by your communication skills.

The challenges we face in our relationships, and keeping our partners happy, are largely determined by our communication skills. The biggest complaint in intimate relationships is that the other person doesn't share their feelings more willingly. A strong second is having difficulty asking your partner for what you want. Other problems are not feeling that your partner understands how you feel; that your partner won't discuss issues, and your partner makes comments that put you down.

When a couple has been together for a while, they begin to make assumptions. Many couples fall into a pattern of thinking that they know each other. They stop asking q uestions. They fail to realize that people change and they may be making a false assumption about them. This can lead to a decline in good communication patterns in your relationship. Early in relationships we tend to look for the positives in each other and overlook the negative qualities. But as time passes, we begin to acknowledge the negative qualities. If we begin to focus on the negative q ualities, we start to make negative "put down" comments. This creates problems. So an important step to take to avoid this is to focus on good qualities and praise your partner for those things often. Try to give your partner compliments every day.

Another important step to take to improve good communicati

on is to make sure to listen and not judge the other person. After listening to what they say, tell your partner what you heard before you respond. Try to suspend an emotional reaction until you are sure you understood them correctly. Another aspect to this is being able to be assertive in the right way in your communication. When an "I" statement is used instead of a "you" statement blame is taken out of the statement and the recipient of the statement is less likely to get defensive.

Of all the things you can do to make your relationship better, these kinds of things will have the greatest impact because communication is the most important skill you need to make your partner happy with your relationship.

Relationship

Advice

How to Be the King of Dating, Sex, Relationship, and Marriage with Secret Tips to Seduce the Love of Your Life and Keep Him or Her for Forever

Part-2

Samantha Gilbert

to date, and reliable, complete information. No warranties of any kind are declared or implied. Readers acknowledge that the author is not engaging in the rendering of legal, financial, medical or professional advice. The content within this book has been derived from various sources. Please consult a licensed professional before attempting any techniques outlined in this book.

By reading this document, the reader agrees that under no circumstances is the author responsible for any losses, direct or indirect, which are incurred as a result of the use of information contained within this document, including, but not limited to, — errors, omissions, or inaccuracies.

Relationship Advice

INTRODUCTION

Have you been looking for love in all the wrong places and in too many faces; only to find more pain and despair?

Then it is time to find out the truth regarding your search for true love.

You don't need to engage in an endless search for Mr. or Mrs. Right, nor do you settle or compromise for any Mr. or Mrs. Right now. If you continue to search for Mr. or Mrs. Right you will inevitably lose yourself trying to please others who can never really be pleased.

When you engage in trying to satisfy the unappeasable you are doing nothing more than giving them the power to control your life. Of course the powerful one is the subtle redeemer of all your good deeds, and can effortlessly play the game all day long everyday. It's much more important to empower yourself by knowing where your love really exists, than it is to be drained of your energy or continue to feel betrayed and end up abandoned by continually giving to someone who is not giving back to you.

Instead of surviving in the lack of love where you find yourself alone, you turn your precious love and attention towards the person who most deserves it, you! So that you can become very consciously aware of any inner healing that is necessary to occur within you that has caused you to invest so much of yourself without any returns.

True Love is the remembrance and moment-to-moment application and expression of self-love. This honors the value of you, your divine magnificence.

You will want to attend to you to be sure you eliminate anything inside of you that is causing you to attract those outer relationships that are less than honorable, respectful and loving. Your healing can occur quickly; as when you are engaged in paying attention to the true love of self, your heart opens and is willing to receive.

The difficulty for most in accepting and acknowledging their own true love is due to the painful experiences from past lives and the past in this life. These experiences are encoded on a cellular level within you. You fear being fully open with your freedom of expression of self on all levels, not just due to the old painful experiences, but at the real causal level originating from when you first chose to lower your vibration to digress into matter, human form when you subscribed to incorrectly believing you are unworthy of true love.

When you incarnate, you came in with a veil of forgetfulness. You are not conscious of this veil, and thusly, you sense a separation from your source, God/Goddess.

In human form you have an ego, or the lower mental mind. This lower mental mind does not have the capacity of understanding like the universal higher mind does. The lower mind attempts to calculate and figure everything out rather than simply connecting to the inner feelings of love.

The lower mind attempting to figure out the sensation of separation, reasons that you must have done something wrong, and your abandonment is a direct punishment for your incorrectly perceived crime. The ego doesn't remember that your soul made the choice to simply experience incarnation for the very purpose of realizing the love it truly is.

Thusly, it calculates if you have done wrong you must be penalized for your wrong doing in some manner. You engage in one life experience after another punishing self in one form or another for doing nothing more than choosing life on earth.

These self-abusing experiences accumulate and compound as you continue to cycle through this incorrect belief of wrong doing punishable by whatever. What you are really unconsciously doing is creating one opportunity after another to be able to see the higher truth of being your own true love. Unfortunately, you as well as many have been stuck in this unhealthy behavior for eons

The self-punishment does have a silver lining, as a result of your multiple painful experiences, you can realize the greater truth that states you have done no wrong, the truth that states you can do no wrong because you are and have always been love. Love that is creating many experiences to realize it is love personified.

The time is now, as this is the Golden age of Heaven on Earth, where all will come to realize the truth of the true love of self.

You need not wait for anyone else to shift your incorrect beliefs into divine knowingness, nor do you need to fear them any longer. For those whom are still not ready to fully awaken to the truth will not be able to get any where near you once you choose love. When you are connected to your true love, you will not encounter these souls, as you have in the past; who are choosing to live in a lower vibration and are stuck in treating others badly because they don't value themselves to begin with.

You need not fear being vulnerable and walking with an open heart, as those who have not yet learned to love themselves simply will not cross your path. The energy of love is a far greater frequency and nothing vibrating from fear will be able to get any where near you. Love cannot encounter fear and those players who are stuck in fear will be on different grounds where they will continue to have the necessary less than loving experiences, so they can come to the same realization of remembering they were never lacking love and need not steal it from another.

When you incorrectly believe you are lacking love, you seek outside of yourself, another person, place or thing that will fulfill and satisfy this sense of lacking. You continue to pursue others one after the other in search of the love you are not willing to give yourself. Sometimes you may play the role of the victim by giving and never receiving equally in return, or you might take on the opposing role of the abuser, where you constantly take without ever being satisfied.

When you play the victim you give anyone and/or everyone the credits for your feel goods and you also project the blame for your feel bads. When you are the abuser you simply blame everyone for everything therefore righteously licensing your terrible treatment of others.

The ego is insatiable because it thrives on the sense of lack; lack is what fuels its fires and thusly you give the power to the ego of self, in your endless search of another to fulfill the very love of which you already are.

Until you are willing, as you have always been able, to stay and master the ego and its control over you and your life by realizing you are responsible for all the choices you have made; you will never come to know and live in the bliss of true love.

Your true love is you!

It does not exist outside of you. The one that exists outside of you is known more commonly as, the conscious life partner or twin flame. Although you will never enjoy the benefits of this whole relationship either until you realize your wholeness lies within.

How could you expect a whole individual to desire to live with and stand by the side of one who believes they are half a person, or lesser than. It simply cannot occur because the vibratory rates are completely different.

The whole individual is vibrating with a frequency of abundance of love of self and therefore lacks nothing. This individual needs no one, even though they may choose to share their life with another. The half individual perceives they are in lack and therefore is always needy. The half person lives in fear and the whole person lives in love, as stated above love and fear simply cannot encounter one another.

You have already experienced the kind of relationship when two fearful low vibrating individuals get together. These two are like separate halfs attempting to make a whole. They may be very attracted at first, because they are both looking for the same thing, someone to make them whole. Eventually they will unconsciously battle over control of the whole. Often with each half switching roles flipping back and forth from the powerful controlling one to the submissive one.

When you incorrectly believe that you lack something and then engage in attempts to fulfill yourself outside of yourself, you will experience being surrounded by many who seem to not want to give you the time of day. They dismiss your opinion as if it is worthless and they don't return the love you wish to give or have given to them.

Anyone one who believes they are not fulfilled without the other half is holding a lower vibration and cannot realize true love until they heal their incorrect beliefs about being less than love, less than loving, less than lovable and less than loved.

Opposing energies cannot meet and stay together for an extended period of time unless one or both change to vibrate at the same rate of frequency. The higher vibrational person will never encounter the lower vibrational individual unless they are participating in their lives for the purpose of healing. In as such the relationship is only temporary unless the lower vibratory person raises its frequency to love and/or the higher vibratory person lowers it frequency to fear.

You will not realize and walk side by side with that life partner or twin flame and/or peers until you are whole yourself. All those that come across your path are always a reflection of self. They are messengers to radiate back to you who you are in any given moment. You will always be surrounded by those that represent who you presently are, who you were in the recent past and who you are becoming in the near future, as you awaken to the true love of self.

Understanding the mirror those around you are reflecting back to you for your greater good and immediate benefit allows you to disengage yourself from another aspect of the lower mental mind known as judgment. If you are disturbed by someone, look upon them and see what is in within self that is so annoying because you choose not to be willing to see that the behavior of the individual is either something you are presently doing yourself, something you have done in the past, or something you are fearful of doing in the future.

Judgment also works the other way, when you find yourself enamored by someone, it is important for you to understand what you love about them is the same that is within you as well. You just don't see it as clearly when you are looking directly at yourself. When you release judgment of self in the understanding that you are your own true love, you can easily relinquish the debilitating judgment of others as well.

In order to fully realize your true love you must apply self -love; meaning do for self what you so willingly do for so many others. Give to self what you have been expecting or demanding others to give to you. Lovingly place yourself at the head of the line, rather in the rear where there is naught left for you. Place yourself not at the head of the banquet table, but rather in a seat at the round table of worthiness for all, as opposed to crawling at the feet of others scrounging for the leftovers or the crumbs that fall at their feet.

You are a queen or king, a Goddess or God because you are the personification of the love of the higher union that exists within you and you deserve the best of everything, not just the best of a few things or in some cases nothing good at all.

Use some of your money to purchase something for self, even if it is determined useless or frivolous by your logical mind or others. If you don't engage in the heart's desires, profound and or silly, you will surely have to spend the same amount of money or more on something else you were not expecting.

Or you may find yourself in a position to have to spend the same amount or more by surrendering it to a physician to help you heal the body that is reflecting back to you, via some disease or uncomfortable pain, your incorrect beliefs of not being love, loving, loved or lovable.

You may have become angry or resentful because you give and are not given to in return and thusly your body will abscess with poison that is being oppressed within and is seeking an avenue of outlet. Or your heart will be in pain and you will have what is called a heart attack; know the heart does not attack, it is reacting in defense of being ignored by you.

Apply self-love by living your life knowing its value and worth. Life is precious and precious few up until now have fully understood the gift of breath. Most of you allow others to live your life for you because you are in fear of loss of love, attention, safety or some other form of support.

The true love of you is independent and whole; it knows no lack and does not seek anything or anyone outside of self because it is always giving to self. It listens to the heart and follows the direction of what makes you happy. True love lives within a thriving joyful heart, not a fearful lacking mind.

Who cares if others call you a silly heart or a Pollyanna; remember misery loves, company because it lacks the courage to step out above or beyond the crowd or tribe. Misery is ego based, it will very boldly or subtly manipulate to get you to join it.

Your own inner true love is prepared to rescue the heart of you; it will whisk you away on a shining white horse of the spirit of courage. You can gain courage in being your own true love by going with what is right for you, rather than giving your power away to another out of fearful limiting incorrect belief of loss.

In divine support of the true love of self, you are being inspired to be willing to no longer dwell in the pain of the past, but to release the long held emotions that have been oppressed. Emotions are like water; they are energy in motion and if they are not honored, acknowledged and expressed in the moment of feeling them, they then stagnate and become a supportive pool for disease in the heart, mind and body.

There is no one denying you true love, other than you. No one is withholding the relationship you deserve, other than you.

Be yourself and trust your feelings, as they are navigating you to what is right for you so you do not compromise yourself for the false love and attention of another. Your emotions are a gift, they are the messengers within to help us become aware of what we are thinking about our self or any other situation for that matter. If we feel bad, we are having some fearful limited thought. If we feel good we are having an expanded loving thought.

Don't hide behind a smile, for if the feelings behind it are disingenuous, It is not OK to be grinning all the time. Emotions must be expressed; they must be given permission to be released in a healthy manner, regardless of whether they are good feelings or less than desirable feeling. You do this with integrity by honoring the feeling whatever it is in the moment you feel it. To dwell in them or project the responsibility of the feeling on to another is unhealthy, as either leads to more of the same vicious cycle of stuffing the emotion and then drawing an experience to you for which the emotion has a pathway to freedom.

This is the unconscious way and inevitably leads to more pain and frustration, more rejection and abandonment, as emotions also grow if they are contained. They become explosive like bombs because they are being resisted and what you resist will indeed persist and before long you explode in someone's face or you explode all over yourself and then the whole nasty business of believing you are not worthy of love begins again.

All of your life you have been trying to prove your worth by getting someone else to be your true love. There is nothing to prove because you already are the true love you are seeking. This would be humorous if it wasn't so sad and in time you will learn to also laugh about it.

The soul of you holds the mastery of the higher mind and lives in the presence of its own true love, it has no need to prove anything. It is the ego that demands acknowledgement. So in attempting to prove what already is known is a bit like banging your head against the wall and wondering why you are bleeding.

The union of the inner God, Goddess is the true loving relationship you.

They intend to be joined together, yet they need your cooperation to come within for your love rather than continually seeking it outside of yourself from another. Even though you ignore their desire they continuously send you unconditionally loving messages. Yet the ego of you would rather be right in its incorrect belief of being the lesser child of God/Goddess and therefore not deserving of love.

Your ego will crucifies you with its rightful indignations rather than be happy in the truth of being the magnificent child of God/Goddess. It would rather project blame onto another, than take responsibility in its fearful unwillingness to accept the truth and heal. It remains far too busy chasing after some man or woman refusing to be calm and listen to the true love that resides within.

If you want true love, than you focus all of your energy on the strength and courage to honor respect and love self. When we take the action to do this all others treat us with the same love, honor, respect and support.

It can be no other way, as no one can help but give to you what you are already giving to self. It works the opposite as well, if you give little or nothing to self than no others can give to you what you are unwilling to give to self.

Look at the real beauty you are, look beyond the physical into the eyes of true love. Gaze within the eyes of the soul you are and know your true love; this will restore your spirit and reawaken your passion

Your true love will compassionately listen to the victim of you, allowing it to be heard and also to shed its long held tears or anger.

This is when your need to look for love outside of yourself can end, as the victim has been heard and it will cease it's tight control over your life with its relentless insatiable needs and wants, as it will no longer fear giving and/or receiving love. It knows beyond the shadow of a doubt it is true love.

The victim is given its voice in a healthy, safe, loving environment where it is able to express all that it feels. The victim then becomes victorious; it wins and its life is filled with wows rather than being dogged by the woes.

In victory of choosing your value and worth, your aura will be crowned with the beauty, love and light of true love of self for all to see. You will know through the encounters with others, who or what each of them is to you and you will engage with them in the highest love, honor and respect of the true love of them as well.

Surround yourself in self loving images, dress yourself up in self loving apparatus and continue to look into the mirror directly into the eyes the windows of the soul and you will see your true love and when you are willing to see this clearly and live it each and every moment, that other if you still desire him or her, whom also knows and is practicing true love can stand with you and for you as an e qual life partner.

You will live in a relationship where there is no blame, no control or any other form of abuse. You will walk in heaven on earth hand in hand in love with self thereby having more than enough love to share with another.

Your heart will be ablaze with the passion for life, as opposed to an endless search for love. You will fully know the value of yourself and the gift you are.

Relationship Advice

RELATIONSHIP COUNSELING

Modeling Relationship Success

We live in a society that places a lot of value on having relationships, but very little value on maintaining strong and healthy relationships. Divorce rates have soared, and fewer couples even bother to get married to avoid the nastiness of divorce. Over all, the quality of relationships have spiraled downward, and so much of it comes right back to learning to talk to each other without resorting to eye gouging, hair pulling, and storming out the door in a heated rage.

The greatest struggle between the sexes is expectation. Women expect (often) that men can read minds and should act accordingly. Men (often) don't appreciate what women really do and expect that there isn't a problem until after the problem has eroded away the foundation. So now what?

Re-evaluation of the role of both partners in any given relationship is of highest priority to those who wish to remain in their relationship. So often, women tend to see discussions as criticism while men take it as complaining. Discussion, believe it or not, is nothing more than the exchange of information. Information that is reasonably exchanged on the job just tells you how to do your job better. Information that comes from your partner is really just information that tells how to do that job better. If we could learn to look at relationship discussions as an exchange of information for the intention of creating a better relationship, half of our problems would easily blow away.

Times have changed and thus our old role models for a good relationship (assuming we ever had them) are no longer applicable. In fact, men who react or act in the same manner as their father or grandfather would be lucky to even find a woman to date, let alone marry. Women have a whole new set of expectations and yet we keep comparing them to our mothers. It really doesn't work well that way. Men were once expected to work hard, come home to a clean house with a warm meal and become the focal point of attention for the rest of the evening. Women have taken a pretty big bite out of the career apple and aren't home all day to live around that expectation. Time for more changes.

Negotiation skills, the ability to exchange information, and the understanding that both parties work hard and both have to share in the rewards as well as the work is a good place to start. Men, a job description for you might read along the lines of: Good communication and negotiation skills are required as job entails ample verbal communication as well as physical communication. Applicant should be able to cut grass, wash dishes, change diapers, and grab their handy drill just as easily as they should be able to provide a steady income, learn to laugh more and talk without yelling.

Women, your job description would resemble: Ability to speak one's mind is a must. Ability to relax about tasks left undone for a day is a huge bonus. Tearful manipulation will not lead to a promotion but the ability to express concerns calmly will. Must be willing to write checks for the bills as easily as whip out a credit card for fun purchases. The ability to learn from conversations will assist the productive outcome faster than dramatic representation of material that only goes on your head.

Relationships are not easy, but well worth the effort when it comes down to it. Taking the time to really hear each other, negotiate better terms, and of course, accept their partner's limitations is a job description that is bound to lead to tenure and happy raises.

Relationship Advice: Marriage Counseling for a Healthy Relationship

How do you know when it's time for marriage counseling? Easy. Are you in a relationship, even a good one? Then it is time.

Years ago my wife and I participated in an organization called "Marriage Encounter," which emphasized communication techniques. I've always liked its motto: "Making Good Marriages Even Better!"

That's what I hope to emphasize for you today. It's time to make your good relationship even better!

And how do I suggest you do that? If you have a relationship that is doing pretty good and doesn't really need any help, then I want you to go to Marriage Counseling!

You may think that counseling is only for problems, but that's not so. People without all those nasty problems can use the process to create far better lives than they ever imagined.

I so love it when a couple comes to me just to grow. I'll admit that this is usually not the case. It usually takes pain to get people through my office door. But, occasionally, couples come to me just to make their good relationship even better. What fun that is!

So, what does a couple do in therapy if they have no problems to work on? There are SO many things we can do:

- ❖ **-Develop even more sophisticated communication abilities**

-Use psychological instruments (tests) to determin differences, simularities, and how to complement each other's personality gifts

-Seek spiritual growth together

Take time out from the busy-ness of life and become clear on what your common goals are and how you want to get there

-Strategize how you will handle holiday get-togethers with in-laws and other relatives that are not that pleasant to be with

And this is just the beginning. There is so much we can do to improve these marvelous relationships we've been given.

Is it worth the cost? I think of it in terms of the old q uestion at the end of life: Will you wish you had spent more time at work, or more time on your family and marriage?

For most of us, the answer is clear. There is nothing in the end more important than our relationships to the people we treasure.

The cost of taking yourselves to a counselor and working on life together is really nothing compared to the lifetime of joy and wonder that is possible with your partner.

The grocery bill, the car payments, the mortgage, the clothes for the kids and the thousands of other things we feel we must spend our money on will all argue against this couple counseling opportunity.

However, I suggest that it is not an issue of whether you can afford it, but whether you can afford to not do it. Is your relationship really good enough for you, or do you wonder if there is more?

Go for it! Grab all the love and togetherness you can get! And use a counselor to help you see what you may be missing.

Hypnotherapy For Building Happy Relationships

There are the happy moments in relationships when two people decide to become a couple, when they decide that they want to stay together, when they both want to commit to each other. They consider themselves happy, perhaps there is an engagement, they decide to marry or they are newly married, or perhaps they just moved in together and started living as a couple. Life feels great, they are loved and they love, and they start building their new life together. They see it as a serious relationship, the beginning of a happy life.

And this is also very often a time when unexpected relationship issues start happening. This could be an unreasonable jealousy, anger, lack of communication, just mentioning a few. Surprisingly, when partners become closer, they may start fighting, they may become demanding, it may seem that the other person is controlling, not caring enough or over protective, too serious or not having any sense of humor. Sometimes there is just a growing anxiety, feeling trapped, feeling insecure. The intimacy weakens, sex is becoming difficult.

152

Sometimes the person can become so upset and disappointed, that he/she employs other coping mechanisms, like drinking, binge eating, insomnia, even some psychosomatic problems. How can all this happen?

When we are more engaged in the relationship, when it is not a flirt or play anymore, when it becomes more important and serious, and we are committed, and we want it to work, we became also more insecure. The deep love may be very frightening. There could be many reasons. First, there can be hurt and resentment from the previous relationships. If the previous fiancé was cheating with your best mate, it is quite likely that you will become jealous in the next relationship. If your previous husband was violent and controlling, you may be inclined to think men are violent and controlling. It seems impossible to trust, even if we are conscious that these fears and assumption are illogical.

There could also be deeper reasons, almost always unconscious. We repeat patterns from our family of origin, we are entangled in the old beliefs and interpretations from childhood and we project those beliefs onto our partners. We very often seek in a partner a substitute for a mother or father, trying to win the parents love from the partner. Sometimes it is opposite; we see a parent's faults in our partner. Mother was controlling and critical, so wife is accused of being controlling and we cannot swallow any criticism from her. Father was violent, so we cannot trust any men. Parents were fighting and not happy, so we can not believe in happy relationships. The family patterns may repeat generation after generation.

The good news is that we do not need to carry the baggage from the previous relationships and from our parents. We can free ourselves from all unhelpful beliefs on a conscious and subconscious level. We can restore the natural flow of love in our families and we can free and empower ourselves. We can create strong lasting relationship, built on love, trust and understanding, and we can grow and evolve together with our partner, letting in the natural happiness and joy in our lives.

There are many approaches aimed at building a loving, lasting relationship. The most common counseling or psychological approach will teach you how to communicate, how to deal with different situations, how to show your feelings. You can learn cognitive and behavioral skills, recognize your thinking patterns, watch and try to control your thoughts, even learn to deal with emotions. Very useful skills, it all helps, even if it may take long a time and a lot of goodwill on both sides.

However , there are better approaches, working on the deepest level, creating real changes, removing all blockages, creating acceptance and understanding, opening the heart and letting the love flow naturally. When there is acceptance and love, there is nothing to hide, there is no reason to control thoughts or deal with emotions, the communication flows naturally, sometimes even without words.

One of the most efficient therapies to work on both conscious and subconscious level is hypnotherapy. It combines counseling and many psychotherapy approaches. The therapy is performed in hypnosis, so the subconscious mind can be explicitly accessed and cleared from unhelpful beliefs and habits. Hypnotherapy allows the most personalized approach. Everybody is different, the web of causes and effects is different for everybody, and in hypnosis the client can access and implement the best solution from the deepest self.

Family Constellations (or Systemic Constellations) is the other powerful phenomenological, alternative or complementary therapy that is gentle, effective and safe. This is an experiential, spiritual and practical approach to building better relationships and reaching your potential. I usually combine the Family Constellation approach with hypnotherapy, together with other techniques, and I've found it one of the most effective methods for restoring the natural flow of love. The Family Constellation workshop allows to reach the deepest possible level of our being,

is even more powerful than the hypnosis, the real movement of the souls is created, real turning point in our lives.

Love Test - What Are the Best Fighting Skills For a Happy Relationship?

Do you avoid fighting with your partner at all costs? Or do you fight often and over the same old issues? You're about to discover why both extremes are a threat to your relationship. And learn how to stop destructive fighting and put up a good fight to create a positive, passionate connection with your romantic partner when you use these smart fighting tips.

What Makes a Guy Fall in Love

Most of us tend to have our own theories regarding what makes a guy fall in love. Based on these theories we change, modify or fine-tune our own attitudes and behaviors so that we fit his requirements to the tee. Alas! More often than not, we miss the target by a mile. The man of our dreams simply walks away for another woman. If the same has happened to you too, it is time to understand that you have made a critical error in your judgment as you are simply clueless about what makes a guy fall in love. To aim right, you have to delve deeper into male psyche. Only then can you achieve success in winning the heart of the man you love.

Come to think of it, there are several factors behind what makes a guy fall in love, many of which depend on what he is looking for in a woman. The need for control, love, power, inclusion, friendship, affection differs widely amongst male mindsets. While some men are enamored by beauty, some crave for grey matter in the woman. Some look for fine legs, some may be very satisfied with someone who is slightly overweight. Be that as it may, there are some common attributes in a woman, which most men find attractive.

Honesty tops the list. During the dating phase, men usually meet women who flaunt their best talents, talk big and go all out to impress the man. This makes honesty take a back seat. However, what makes a guy fall in love is when he meets an honest woman who is devoid of any pretensions, complexities and appears transparent. The important point to note here is that pretensions can take you up to a certain limit and not beyond that. Therefore if you are seriously attracted to someone and pondering over what makes a guy fall in love, as well as stay in love with you, be honest to him as well as to yourself. Your relationship can then take off on a firmer and more trusted ground.

The next important attribute that makes up for what makes a guy fall in love is the level of self confidence that you exude. A woman can appear demure, shy or reticent - but should never be in doubt. What makes a guy fall in love the moment he sets his eyes on her is when he is mesmerized by the way she carries herself. Every man loves the woman to depend on him emotionally but never make the mistake of clinging on to him for your emotional needs. Such emotional dependence usually scares a man away. Be firm and decisive without appearing overbearing or selfish. Have a definite point of view but remain flexible to accept his views too.

What makes a guy fall in love with a woman is when he sees traits in the woman that he admires and respects. Things like jealousy, possessiveness, exclusivity, etc are good to the extent that they are present in limited and measured doses. But if you appear confident, in total control of your emotions, you can have the man licking out of your hands in no time. What makes a guy fall in love with you is when he knows you are attracted to him but are willing to give him that space. In other words, never overwhelm him with your love and attention - as these usually suffocate a man. What makes a guy fall in love and stay in love with you is when you are different from the rest he has met so far!

Because a good relationship is one of the most treasured of human interactions. We all want to be loved. There are the great times together, the shared dreams and visions, the mutual likes and dislikes and more. Great relationships are essential for enjoying a good quality of life. They color everything else around us.

Losing a lover is one of the most emotionally traumatizing episodes in our life. It is amazing how the very thing that brings us the most pleasure also brings with it the most grief.

But your situation is not hopeless. Actually, it is far from it. It is quite possible to win your ex back regardless of whether they eloped with someone else or not. I have successfully done it myself and you can do it too. Of course, you have to know how to do it effectively.

What's the danger in avoiding a fight?

Dr. Ellyn Bader said the dictionary defines fighting as defeating your adversary. She said a better definition of fighting in a relationship is working through issues with honesty and compassion.

Dr. Peter Pearson warned that couples who avoid tough issues may cause all passion to erode over time, because neither partner will risk bringing up a stressful topic. Boring, safe conversations about the weather or the menu can suck the excitement out of a relationship.

The antidote is to take a risk and face issues that cause you pain while you find the solution with mutual compassion for each others needs and well being. This deepens your emotional connection and builds trust.

How do some couples get stuck in a fighting rut?

When couples are always ready for a fight or they keep having the same fight that doesn't go anywhere, Dr. Pearson says their brain often is to blame.

He explained that people who have been exposed to painful and threatening life experiences in childhood actually store these painful feelings in their inner brain, the amygdala, also known as the emotional brain. Whenever a new experience matches an old painful one, these triggers cause the wounded emotional brain to start a fight and protect you from more pain.

One antidote is to use relaxation or biofeedback techniq ues to ease the stress of these triggers. The smell of Cloves also can calm your emotional brain's urge to fight.

Dr. Pearson said these tools won't help you stop a fight while you're in one.

How do you stop a fight quickly?

Dr. Bader suggested you take a breather and say to yourself, "It's not about me, it's about them--about something that upset them in the past." As you consider their old issues, it helps you feel compassionate understanding of your partner.

Dr. Bader and her husband also use the "Ouch Exercise" to stop a fight. You have to plan it in advance so that you know what words hurt you and what words would make you feel better if your partner said them to you.

When your partner is using words that hurt you at the start of a fight, the goal is to calmly say, "Ouch--can we replay it again?"

This is a signal for your partner to calm down. Then you tell your partner the words that hurt you, and you say the words you want to hear instead because this would help you feel better.

Dr. Pearson said this gets you out of the victim brain. It is soothing to repeat these requested words a few different ways. Dr. Bader said she advises couples to become curious instead of furious.

How?

For example, if your partner comes home without doing what they had promised to do and they start making excuses, then you would use the "Ouch-replay" script to stop the fight and rewrite the script.

You could tell your partner that you'd feel better if they'd apologize for not keeping their promise, and maybe other promises.

Your partner will calmly say what you requested. Ideally, this gives them an understanding of how their words and actions affect you, and vice versa. This healthy communication builds a happy relationship.

If your partner refuses to stop fighting or learn the skills to increase healthy communication, it would be difficult to improve your relationship which dims prospects for a happy, healthy connection.

What if you're single? Should you test your date's fighting skills before you commit to a serious relationship?

Dr. Pearson suggested you ask your date how they feel about disagreements or how they might bring up issues that bother them. Then you can reach an agreement of how you would deal with differences if you decide to enter a long-term relationship.

How to Determine If Marriage Counseling Will Save Your Relationship

Many married couples who are struggling in their relationships consider seeking professional advice from a marriage counselor, but still they hesitate. From stories they've heard, they wonder if counseling really works.

Besides, they hate to spend money on this type of resource unless they have assurance that they will reap rewards for their investment. So the questions remain. What exactly should they expect from counseling sessions, and will they be able to save their relationship and build a stronger union?

Every marriage has its problems, and it's unrealistic to expect yours to always be smooth sailing. What couples need to learn are strategies that can help them weather the bad times, open lines of communication, and stay happily married. They need to discover techniques that will enable them to deal with the perceived shortcomings they see in their spouses and reach compromises about how they are going to live together peacefully and lovingly. When you visit a marriage counselor, you get the opportunity to open up honest communication which is key to a stable relationship. You will learn from an unbiased third party how you can go about arguing over your issues in a much healthier manner.

No two marriages are the same, so obviously marriage counseling isn't going to be as effective for some partners as it is for others. Yes, there's a chance that you may end up deciding on divorce even with the counseling; however, it will certainly give you a better chance of reconciling your differences and saving your marriage than doing nothing will. At the first signs your marriage is in trouble, you should seek guidance from a marriage counselor, because your marriage will be easier to save in the early stages than it will be later on. Not that you can't benefit when things have already gotten bad between you, but it's far better to get an early start.

There are other factors that will help determine how successful marriage. It's easier to resurrect a failing marriage in which the partners are both young and still in love than it is to save a more long-term marriage in which the couple has grown out of their relationship and so far apart that the love is buried much deeper. In addition, both members of the partnership need to be willing to cooperate with the counselor and each other if real progress is going to be made. Other couples that may not be as successful in counseling include people who married very young and before their relationship had a chance to mature, high school dropouts, people whose parents are divorced, those in inter-cultural marriages, those who live below the poverty level, or those who are unemployed.

What Is Premarital Counseling? It's Not As Scary As You Might Think

Premarital counseling is a specialized form of counseling that is dedicated to preparing engaged couples for marriage.

Premarital counseling is typically done by a licensed therapist, clinical social worker, coach or religious leader.

Why choose it?

There are many great reasons for experiencing premarital counseling. People who are from divorced families may want to ensure that they are fully prepared for the realities of marriage. Couples who want to focus on preventing destructive problems from developing in the first place may want to work on essential relationship skills. People who value exploring psychological issues may opt to participate in premarital counseling in order to make sure that they understand their own and their partner's motivations for marriage. And some couples choose premarital counseling because they are required to do it in order to get married.

What should you expect?

You should expect a safe space to explore the strengths and challenges of your relationship and your backgrounds. Premarital counseling is often focused on building on the strengths of a couple, learning techniques to prevent problems, and learning skills. This makes it very different than individual counseling - where the focus is generally on a particular problem or difficulty managing a phase of life.

What kind of topics are typically discussed?

Premarital counseling sessions can focus on a wide range of topics depending on the style and preferences of the counselor that you choose. However, most premarital counseling generally focuses on a few core areas. These are the topics that generally trip up even the best marriages from time to time, so it is especially important to work through any difficulties in these areas before marriage.

Typical premarital counseling topics include the following:

Communication

As you can imagine, communication issues top the gripe list of many marriages - even good marriages. So, most premarital counselors will want to get to know how you communicate as a couple. The counselor will probably not only ask you questions about the history of communication in your relationship, but will also observe how you communicate in person. If you are nervous about the idea of someone else observing your interactions as a couple, then perhaps try doing some work in the privacy of your own home related to improving communication. If you do decide to go to premarital counseling - good for you - because the counselor is likely to make some useful recommendations for ways that you can communicate better with your partner.

Conflicts and Conflict Resolution

Ask any married couple which skills they would like to improve in their marriage - and I guarantee a significant portion will say, "conflict resolution skills." So, of course, premarital counseling will also focus on this key area of any intimate relationship. You probably can't imagine it right now (because chances are you are an engaged person deeply in love with your partner) but there will come a time when you will probably be surprised at how much you can dislike someone that you love so much! That's where conflict resolution comes into the picture. So, in premarital counseling you will learn essential skills for managing conflicts that are inevitable in any long-term intimate relationship.

Financial Values

Be ready to also talk about money in premarital counseling. Money issues are one of the top three reasons why married couples end up separating. So, exploring your financial values and whether or not you are both on the same page regarding your short term and long term financial goals is crucial. Planning a wedding together can often be the first time couples are really faced with sorting out their different financial values, so discussing any issues you are having in this area with your premarital counselor is an excellent idea. This is especially true if you find yourself bickering over what to spend money on for wedding. An inability to sort out your differences now spells inevitable conflicts in the future.

Cultural Values

If you and your partner are from different cultural or racial backgrounds then these differences are likely to show up in expected and unexpected ways. Premarital counseling is the perfect place to discuss these differences. If you and your partner are different in any of these ways then you are probably already aware of the ways that these differences can play out in wedding planning. Because even if you are both pretty flexible around traditions, it may not be the case that your parents are so flexible in this regard. And things get even trickier if children enter the picture! So, taking the time to discuss your different values in premarital counseling can set the tone for your marriage in terms of being able to delve into your differences in respectful ways.

Religious Values

You are likely to explore any differences you may have related to your religious beliefs and values during premarital counseling. This is of course even more likely if you choose to go to a religious leader for counseling. So, this can be a time that you both figure out the role of religion in both of your lives and the ways that you both envision practicing (or not practicing) your respective faiths. The impact of religion on marriage is not to be underestimated. Research has shown that when two people of different faiths marry, they are more likely to end up divorcing. This is probably related to the role that religion plays in managing stress. If the members of the couple use religion in very different ways then it may create a barrier between them during an already stressful situation. But more research needs to be done in this area to make any conclusive statements. But the take home message is this: if you marry someone with different religious beliefs then your own take the time to plan for how these differences will be managed before life gets too stressful!

Family Histories

Premarital counseling is also a time when you will explore your family history with your partner. Now this doesn't mean that you have to share all kinds of family secrets and disgraces with your partner - your partner will more than likely learn about these things over time. But it is a time to explore the really important issues like important family dynamics (for example, the impact of divorce on your family) or whether an important illness has shaped your family functioning (for example, an alcoholic parent or a sibling with a mental illness). This is a time for your partner to begin to understand who you are in a deeper and more fundamental way. And most importantly you can discuss a plan for managing how these things will affect your marriage.

Relationship History

If you've been married before or were in a long-term relationship that impacted you in profound ways then you can use the space within premarital counseling to discuss your relationship history. Now keep in mind that your partner is not likely to want to hear all about the details of your previous relationship - so it is not the time to work through any unresolved issues you may have (use personal therapy for that!). But it is a time to address any issues that may come up regarding your relationship history in a matter of fact way. This is of course especially important if there are children from your previous relationship in the picture.

How to Build Trust Back in a Relationship

Relationship experts point out that the secret ingredient on how to build trust back in a relationship is for the couple to achieve stability. In recently reconciled partners, trust is very volatile since there can still be the "past cheating" air floating around. But if the couple aims not to build trust first but stability in the relationship, then the virtue of trust follows. Working on the six mainstays of a stable relationship creates a strong bond of trust between the couple.

The following are the six mainstays of a stable relationship. Achieving each of these in a gradual process will persuade trust back into one's relationship.

The Six Mainstays of a Healthy, Stable Relationship

1. Communication.

Talking with each other is an intimate gesture (aside from sex) that will hold the bond of two couples together. Being open, honest, and consistent in communicating with each other helps a lot in repairing gaps. On the other hand, do set parameters before any conversation as this will help in preventing "resolved" past issues from being dug up again in case the 'simple chat' becomes heated up.

2. Consistency.

If the couple had just recovered from an issue of affair, it is quite difficult to establish a consistent pattern of talking and communicating with each other again. That is why each couple should make sure that they have a "chat time" with each other on a regular basis. This is an important aspect of learning how to build trust back in a relationship.

3. Resolving Conflict.

Conflicts can also be good; it is a sign that both the husband and the wife care about their relationship that they want to express their ideas. However, conflicts must be settled before it turns into major disagreements. When the tension heats up during a conflict, it is advisable for both parties to take a time out. RELAX, and get back to the discussion when they're both pacified.

4. A Healthy Sex-Life.

Sex is part of the couple's need for intimacy. After an infidelity issue, it is advisable for the couple to talk about sex and how they can both find out ways to satisfy each other in bed again.

5. Having Fun Together.

It is usually difficult for a couple to have fun together right after a recent affair because the feeling of being uncomfortable takes away the fun part in everything. This is normal, but the two must not wait too long. The couple must start having fun with each other: go to movies, take a new adventure, play games, etc. If one partner feels happy with the other, it can spark the good relationship back again and is an integral step when understanding how to build trust back in a relationship.

6. Integrity.

Integrity in this sense means that the couple must keep their commitment with each other intact, complete and undivided. Working on one's integrity is a gradual process, but as time passes, it becomes stronger and more stable.

Issues of trust have always been at the forefront of most couples relationships, especially if a recent affair had just wreaked the trust in a relationship apart. Building that trust back again is quite a challenge, but experts say, it's not that impossible. These six stability pillars can help establish the foundation of trust in a newly reconciled couple. Working hand in hand, and finding ways on how to build trust back in a relationship can help couples find their relationship on track again.

If you feel that the trust has gone from your relationship, you can get immediate help right now.

The Main Reasons Why Long Distance Relationships Don't Work

I would like to tell you that this is not going to give you reasons why you should not get into a long distance relationship. You should be aware that distance relationships can work and often do work. It takes quite a lot of effort for you to to gain a good outcome, but the results are excellent. You will find listed below the major reasons that a distance relationship may not be successful.

❖ A Variation of Expectations

People often have no idea on what it means to be in a distance relationship. Many presume it's a chance to be free of their lovers chains for some time. While others might think it will be an unfortunate tragedy. Both of you have got to be aware that this could possibly be harder than you think. But don't be intimidated. Just like we said, the rewards can be great.

❖ The Cost of Flights/ Gasoline

In case you're lucky enough to reside in the same country, or perhaps the same state or county, as your partner you probably may only have to pay for a train or bus pass to visit with them. However if your long distance sweetheart is overseas, you should definitely keep the traveling costs in mind.

Not Enough Interaction

Bear in mind that you need to stay in close contact with your partner. It is often advised by a relationship counsellor that regular couples ought to spend eight hours alone with the other every week. And the same is recommended for distance couples. It can be quite difficult when you each have separate careers and life plans to keep up this communication. Also when the early "love-struck" thoughts have worn off, chatting through a laptop may begin to get fairly dreary. We recommend that you plan some great long distance dates.

❖ Loss of Trust

Trust is the number one reason that a distance relationship won't work. Many have a false presumption that they are able to do anything they want when their significant other is away. We highly advise against this perception. Taking part in trust activities and asking partnership building questions to get to know each other better will really help to build a solid foundation of trust.

❖ Different Views

Two opposites won't remain together if the both of you have totally different views on important factors of life. Prior to starting a distance relationship you need to make time to talk about each others opinions. And just remember that it can save a relationship to change your opinions to meet your lovers.

❖ Absolutely No Future Plans

The primary reason why the majority of relationships go wrong - not to mention the distance ones - is because there are simply no plans for the long term. Be sure to clearly establish where the relationship is going before you depart. This should save a ton of grief along the line.

How do I help myself to improve my health and sex life

If you are going through the menopause and have come to this page looking for help for such an intimate problem as dry sex or a dry vagina during sex then we may be able to help you. It may be that you are too embarrassed to speak to your husband, friend or doctor. If so, then stay here and be among friends. You are not on your own.

Have you tried all of the (menopause) creams in the market only to find that just as you are starting to enjoy yourself in that intimate time of lovemaking, that the cream has dried up and the intimacy is now painful?

You are not alone.

Millions of pre-menopausal, menopausal and post menopausal (menapause) women have a similar experience of a dry vagina, or no lubrication before or during sexual intercourse

Some women will allow this condition to send them to a life of celibacy, withdrawing from any sexual encounters- the "I have a headache" syndrome. Unfortunately, this behaviour impacts severely on the relationship, which in turn will impact on the family. This can result from arguments set up by the woman to draw the attention away from herself thus trying to make herself undesirable to her husband or partner. (Sound familiar?)

The next path taken is that the husband or partner, who simply cannot understand the complex issues of being a woman, may begin to venture elsewhere to have his sexual needs met. Thus the family component is compromised and begins to shatter into pieces.

Unless a quick solution is found to rectify the problem before it gets to this stage, the relationship can spiral out of control.

So, what may be an effective solution?

In our Western world, the common form of management of menopausal symptoms is still the traditional method of visiting your doctor who will most likely prescribe medication in the form of unnatural hormone replacement therapy. It is important to understand that chemical or artificial forms of hormone can be dangerous over a length of time. Many times, women will be asked to stop their hormone replacement therapy course mid course through management so that the woman does not risk the development of heart disease or cancer! The very illnesses that the course is meant to prevent.

By helping women to feel confident about looking for natural alternatives to HRT or Hormone Replacement

Therapy, women are becoming more open about what they want and what they DON"T want. Educated women who have taken steps to educate themselves about their own body, might be surprised to find that there is no technical or medical word for Menopause in the Asian languages.

Why? It has been found that women in Asia consume vast amounts of green leaf vegetables, high in chlorophyll and phyto-estrogens. These naturally occurring phyto-estrogens mimic the real human estrogens thus helping women to retain their hormonal levels whilst their bodies go through the cessation of their periods and they transition into maturing women of non-reproductive age.

Understanding that menopause may actually not be a naturally occurring phenomena but an artificial one built from a modern world of poor nutrition and lack of fresh fruit and vegetables, may help women to take better control of their bodies, their future and their sexuality.

Relationships and Technology

Choice is not always a blessing. As it has often been said, "with choice comes responsibility."

I recently went on a weekend road trip to a hot springs retreat center in a very remote location. As my husband and I started to drive on the dusty and winding road, cell phone reception worsened and, within moments, the words "No Service" flashed on my phone screen. Every time I glanced over at my smart phone and saw the two words, I felt a strange mix of nervousness and joyful relief.

I had no service and no choice. "To tech" or "not to tech" was not the question.

My lack of choice made me acutely aware of the choice we do have in our daily lives. It reminded me of the daily myriad of decisions many of us, technology users, face every day at home or while with love ones. We mostly have the choice, conscious or not, to decide if or when to fire up our computers, to switch our phones on or off, to turn to our gadgets... or to our partners.

The Impact of Technology on Relationships

Decades ago, this type of choice was not as imperative, or as relevant. However, technology use has become so pervasive that if we fail to consciously exercise our power of choice today, the automatic impact of technology on relationships will choose for us. The mesmerizing power of the gadget will prevail.

A new Telenav study revealed that a third of Americans would prefer to give up sex for a week, rather than their cell phones. A recent British study by Ikea showed that couples are spending more time in bed looking at laptops than looking at each other. According to a report by Spring Technology, an IT recruitment company, "70 per cent agree that checking work emails while on holiday damages relationships." You get the idea.

We are becoming so dependent on our gadgets that relationships are increasingly taking the backseat.

Choose Consciously

Whatever the origin of that impulse to turn to tech rather than to each other, it comes with a cost. Relationships need to be fed to stay healthy and thrive. Time and attention are fertilizers.

Needless to say, we may need or want to use technology while with our loved ones. Sometimes, technology can bring us closer together. The key, however, is to choose consciously.

So every time you are about to turn to a digital device rather than to your partner, stop and ask yourself these 3 questions:

1) What motivates me to turn to technology in this moment? Need, enjoyment, compulsion, avoidance?

2) Will tech use bring us closer together or further apart right now?

3) Looking back at my life from my death bed, will I have any regrets about my gadget use?

Compatibility and Intimate Relationships

A wise old lady was asked to share her insights on the problem that is inherent with intimate relationships. The wise-m'am was reluctant to do so, but after some prodding she relented by saying, "Only if we can talk openly, where no one is an expert, so we may be able to see the problem unfold before us."

The Wise-m'am was asked, "Where should we begin?"

She proceeded by saying, "We might be better served to begin at the point after the initial attraction between two people, when dating begins the process of romantic, passionate attachment, when the heat of intimate relationship begins. Romance is the match that lights the fire between individuals, but it requires something else to sustain the burn. Is it not important for us to discover what those ingredients are that combine to sustain the relationship burn?"

Someone spoke up and put the question to the Wise m'am regarding, shouldn't we ask what we mean by intimate relationship? Wise-m'am agreed that was a reasonable place to begin.

Wise-m'am went on to suggest, "Relationship seems to imply a connection of, or between, two individuals which serves to bind the participants-is that not the state of affairs as we've come to know it today? It is the process of becoming interrelated into a single unit that is known to us as an intimate relationship. Intimate relationship often has a sexual component attached to it-but not always."

The question was put to Wise-m'am "What do you think is the biggest determining factor to a successful intimate relationship?"

Wise-m'am smiled and said, "Depends on who you ask, but most women would probably say love, many men might say sex-not necessarily good sex-just sex."

The audience chuckled to hear those words coming from such a wise and serous woman.

Wise-m'am continued, "Let us assume-and rightly so-that love is the bedrock for any meaningful intimate relationship. That being said, the one variable after love with the greatest impact to an intimate relationship would have to be the level of compatibility between the respective participants. This relates to traits like a harmonious fit, as well as the level of flexibility, and adaptability of the participants. We should say that there are two critical components to compatibility, and those are the needs, and wants of the participants, and how well they serve their personal interests as well as the interest of the relationship."

"So let us clarify what we mean by need and want. A need can be said to require something essential or indispensable, or require or feel the necessity for something specific. Another way to put it would be to characterize a need as a demand made on the relationships and the participants, such as the need to be honest with one another or to be monogamous."

"Let us now clarify what is meant by want. Couldn't we say that want is rooted in desire or craving? It is the inclination toward something or to have a fondness for something. For example; I want us to spend Sundays together as a family unit, or it could be as simple as I want some ice cream. In the end it comes down to how well the relationship meets the needs and wants of the participants, does it not? It is matter of blending the needs and wants of the individual participants into a combination that is unique to the intimate relationship. So, it appears that what has been revealed to us is that the inherent problem in intimate relationship comes down to the compatibility of the participants. This demonstrates the significance of compatibility, and the quality of the relationship. Do we agree?"

RELATIONSHIP ADVICE-WHAT DOES IT AKE TO BE A MAN

When we are posed with that question many things come to mind. We can talk about confidence, leadership, strength and all of those would be good answers, but what is the core of being a man? In the last 40 years the roles of a man and woman have become more and more blurred. Women in the 1940's and 1950's would stay home, raise the children and took on the role of a submissive wife. In the 1960's and 1970's feminism took center stage and as more and more divorces happened women became single mothers and left to raise boys on their own. I was a product of a single mother and no father in the 1980's and I have spent a great deal of my life trying to answer the question of what does it mean to be a man?

Now as we turn the page into 2010 we see these roles barely exist anymore. Men have become dependent, lacking direction, followers, cowards and more than anything irresponsible. In the community we learn about the "attraction switches." We are taught to be confident but we are never instructed as to WHY this role is important or even HOW to actually sustain confidence.

So what is a man in 2010 and why does this matter to your dating life?

Because being a man is a role that will NEVER disappear. It may seem obvious, but the truth is;

Women... Like... Men..

I want to give you my characteristics of what a man is and what their role is.

Responsibility

Most men believe that being responsible means supporting a family financially. Being responsible means your role is to accept when you are wrong, but live with the mindset that you are right and confident in your ability to make decisions. A man should also contribute to the emotional, spiritual, physical and mental well-being of his family and significant other. This means taking action when the circumstances call for it and doing what it takes to solve issues that arise.

A Protector

A protector means that you can more than just physically protect her from other people; it also means protecting her self-esteem and self-worth. One of the greatest compliments a woman can give a man is to feel safe around him.

A Leader

A good leader takes the lead rather than passively waiting for your spouse or significant other to initiate it. Leadership shows confidence and we all know that confidence is very attracting to a woman. Most guys miss the mark here and view leadership as a one way street. A good leader inspires others to greatness, thus giving value while he leads the relationship or household.

A Mentor

A man of high value is a mentor to others through word and action. Set high standards and teach by doing. He is impeccable with his word and his actions display confidence as well as mentoring others to improve their lives. This is a powerful trait for a man to have because the strength of character it takes to be a mentor shows a wide variety of attraction switches such as: Confidence, leaderships, social proof and social status.

 The spineless behavior of men is changing the roles that men and women have and causing men to become submissive, feminine and afraid to take the lead.

The first step to understanding and changing this behavior is becoming dominant.

Dominance does NOT mean that you own another person, simply put dominance means that you have authority over another person. You take the lead and lead the interaction. If we talk about relationships it means that you are the one who leads the relationship, others are along for the ride and offer their input. You do NOT control the other person, she is free to be who she is just as you are free to be who you are, you are simply leading the relationship and she is more than welcome to add input.

A lot of guys mistake dominance for total control...

A relationship is not about control because control is based in fear, a relationship should be founded on love and love is all about freedom. Dominance simply means that you are going to step up and be the man. You are going to lead her and she is going to choose to follow or not. This means making plans, choosing where to eat, setting boundaries and enforcing them.

The next step is Assume leadership.

You are the leader because you are the man. Tell her what you want!! When I counsel people in a relationship I often find the same issue that happens over and over again. Neither person is expressing what they actually want.

You will NEVER get what you want if you do not clearly communicate what you actually want and expect from the other person.

Assuming leadership means that you understand your role as the man in the relationship is to step up and lead. Take authority over your actions and lead the relationship where you want it to go.

Controlling Emotions

One quality of a man that many people overlook is the ability to control emotions. Women are creatures of emotion and thus their moods will change as their emotion's change. As a man you are responsible for controlling your emotions and not letting your emotions control you. Many times when a man has no father figure and was raised by a mother only he will be a very emotional man. Part of assuming the role of a man though is to have dominance over your emotional well-being as well. Its OK to show emotions, in fact it is vital! However, you need to show restraint and that restraint of emotion is VERY attractive to women.

Becoming Independent

Independence is a major trademark of a man. Independence shows that you can take care of yourself and therefore you can take care of others. Independence shows that you understand the way life works and have broken free from your dependence on others both financially and emotionally.

Having Direction in life

Having a direction in life is another vital role that a man must take on. If you are to be the leader of a relationship or family you must display that you are taking her in a direction she wishes to go and that she has the faith in you to follow. One of the greatest compliments a woman can give a man is that you are multi-dimensional. You have passions other than what she first saw.

Setting standards

In the beginning of any interaction with a woman you are sending signals to each other about where your boundaries are. You communicate these in many ways such as verbal cues, body language and willingness to comply with suggestions. As you set boundaries the woman's job is to test these boundaries to see if you will keep her in check. As the man allows his boundaries to be broken the woman loses attraction for him. Over time, the woman will leave the man because she loses all respect for him and sees him as an unsuitable partner.

A man sets his standards and keeps them there. One of the greatest phrases that holds true in life is "we teach people how to treat us." We do this by setting boundaries and then holding others accountable for violating them.

For a final point I will try to answer the question what does it mean to be a man. I guess from all my experiences I can say that we know we are a man when we see one. When you become responsible for your actions you begin to understand the world not from the eyes of selfishness, but from the eyes of selflessness.

the basic need of a man

With a title like this for a book I am assuming that many of the readers will be women. Curiosity will get the better of the ladies who see the title and may want to know for themselves what someone is saying about men. Many of the women reading this will probably say that men only have two needs. Sex and something cold to drink. That is cruel and heartless ladies. We are not as shallow as we look and act. We have feelings, we can be hurt. Stop laughing.

The 21st Century man has had to make a lot of adjustments. No more getting by with just grunting and muttering. Men have had to learn to be communicators at work, at play and in relationships. That is not to say that men have not always been deep on the inside, but, they've been able to get away with keeping that side of their personalities hidden. No more. The time to reveal our TRUE manhood is now. Are you ready ladies? Do you really want to find out what the basic needs of a man are? Read on and be enlightened. At the end of this book you will look upon the male race with a whole new respect, or at least not laugh as much as you used to. Be kind and patient with us. We are learning and I hope you will learn something about us too. Thanks for reading. (That includes you guys who are reading this in secret because you don't want anyone to think you are a softie.)

The Need to Be Loved

Hard to imagine I know but men really do have a need to be loved. As children men enjoyed receiving love from parents and other family members. They enjoyed being praised and told how special they were. As they got older this need never went away. It didn't show itself as much as the men got in to their teen years and older but deep inside their souls was a voice crying out, "Love me." For some strange reason men acquire this "macho" exterior and try to show an indifference to life. What that means is they try to convey and attitude of steel, that things don't affect them. In reality the opposite is true. Men are affected by all sorts of things that are thrown at them. They get discouraged, embarrassed, hurt, and disappointed. Their insides are churning through all of this but their outer image is one of someone who doesn't care or isn't affected by events.

A guy's heart gets broken just like a woman's. When a girl breaks up with a guy he might cry when he is alone. He probably pines for her and wants to send her sweet love notes or poems but his pride prevents him. All of this started in the Garden of Eden when Adam ate the fruit and then blamed Eve when God came around. Eve may have influenced Adam but he had a choice not to eat the fruit but being a lamebrain he ate it. Once he ate it he knew he was in trouble and immediately looked around for someone else to blame. Eve was nice and handy. Of course she turned around looking for someone to blame and there was only her and Adam so the serpent got the blame. God decided that all three of them were in trouble and kicked them out of the Garden of Eden. Hence you and have to work for a living instead of sitting around all day naming animals and eating fruit. Thanks Adam and Eve, and the serpent too.

Why are men so reluctant to show their need for love? Fear of rejection. Men are afraid of being rejected by their partner, their parents, their friends, their co-workers, and their bosses. Putting on an exterior of toughness helps to prevent pain, or so men think. In reality it only makes the healing process harder as men have more to struggle through to get to healing.

What can men do to overcome the pride issue and admit their need to be loved? They can start by being honest with themselves . Many men have hidden their true feelings to the point they don't even know they have them anymore so they need to face up to the facts and admit to themselves that they have a need to be loved. After that they need to admit it to those they love; their partners, their children, their parents. Once you admit your need for love you become open to receive it. When you are not open to it, guess what? You can't receive it. Hence many men go along in life with a chip on their shoulders or angry all the time, or spiteful or mean. They are not receiving love because they haven't opened themselves to it.

So guys, learn to realize the power of love. The more you have inside you, the more you can give to others. Don't you want to love your partner more? Your kids, your parents, your friends. Only a birdbrain would say no, I don't want to love people more, I am happy being a miserable old sod. Take stock of your life today and open your mind, your heart, and your sprit to a world that may be new to you. A world filled with the capacity to give and receive love. Your whole life will change. Those around you will be happier and will react differently to you from now on. Their happiness levels will increase as will yours. Isn't that something to get excited about?

What about those guys who will close the doors and not be open to this? Unfortunately they will carry on doing what they have always done; act tough, act unaffected by others, pretend they don't have feelings or emotions. They will argue that they have gotten through life fine up until now, why do they need to listen to me? Let me suggest that if you are one of these guys that you take a good, long, hard look at your life up to today. Take a look in every room in your mind and your heart. What do you see? Do you see cleanliness, contentment, happiness? Or do you see emptiness, anger, loneliness, sadness, despair, and striving for acceptance? I would hazard a guess that you have some of those areas still lingering.

Why am I so confident about this? Because I, like all men, have had them in my life too. I have allowed cobwebs to form on the inside of my rooms and not dusted or cleaned them out, resulting in shadows, dark areas, empty areas which needed to be filled with joy but I wouldn't open the doors and let the light and the love in. My loss.

'Don't judge me by what I have done but rather by what I am capable of doing."

Do you want to change? Do you want to become who you really should be? I hope you answer yes. It is for your own sake as well as your loved ones that you need to change and admit your need for love. All men need alone time; all women need alone time. As a guy. you still need your buddies to interact with. None of that needs to change unless it is bad for your most important relationships. The change I am talking about is an internal change in your heart and your mind. A new way of thinking. Learn to thank others for their love. When you come home tomorrow walk up to your partner and thank them for loving you. Thank your children for being your children and for loving you. Tell them how much it means to you have their love in your life. The more you express it the more it will mean to you and the more important it will become in your life. Learn to constantly express love and thanks to those most important to you. Trust me; you will see a lot of changes take place.

When your children feel like they are important to you and they play a major role in your happiness they will become more loving, more committed to you because they will be drawn to your open heart. This in turn will fill your life with joy and happiness. Your outlook on life will change. You will look for opportunities to do things together as a family. Suddenly a night with the boys at the bar won't have near the appeal it used to have. Board game night with the family will become one of the most exciting parts of your week. Don't believe me? Try it and see.

Now you know you have a need for love all you have to do is believe it, admit it, and open yourself to others to receive it and give it. You won't be disappointed

The Need for Quiet

One of the hardest things for women to understand about men is their need for quiet. Because women tend to be more communicative verbally, they assume that if men are being quiet they are not communicating. When quite the opposite is true. Men communicate very often through lack of noise.

If a woman is sitting with her partner in a room and he is q uiet but appears content, rejoice, he is happy. If a man is not happy with his partner or the relationship it will show up in his facial expression and his body language. On the other hand if he is happy that too will show up on his face. By being quiet it is not a reflection on his partner, it actually means he is comfortable around her and can relax and be quiet and just enjoy her presence. Ladies does that sound difficult to understand? Don't worry all will be revealed as we go through this book and by the time we finish men and women will know men like the back of their hands.

Women need to allow men a time for quiet in the relationship. It may be when he is watching TV or reading a book or just lying on a couch with his eyes closed. Ladies, guys hate it when you talk while you are both watching TV or a movie. Men tend to focus on what they are doing at that particular time. If you are watching a movie together he is concentrating on the movie. That is not a good time to expect him to be up for talking about visiting your parents or changes you want to make to your house or apartment.

To truly communicate as a couple you both need to set aside a time every day that is wrap-up time. This time can be used to bring each other up to date on what has happened during your day and how you are feeling. It is also a good time to discuss upcoming activities or any challenges or difficulties either of you feel have crept in to the relationship. Once this time is finished don't expect him to dwell on it too long, he has gone on to ponder other things. A woman on the other hand will ponder it more and analyze the man's body posture, the words he used, the tone he said the words in and try and figure him out. This can cause problems because she can read things in to a situation that are not there.

By allowing the man a time for quiet it shows you respect him as a man and are comfortable with him. This makes him feel appreciated and confirms that the two of you are in sync. Ladies, don't try and analyze this too much. It will be hard for him to explain but he still needs this quiet time. Just enjoy the moments with him. Listen to music on your iPod or read a good book but because you are in the room with him it will feel like you are enjoying each other's company. Men appreciate each other in silence. They don't need to talk a lot to communicate. That is not to make excuses for a man; he does need to express himself more but compromise will go a long way towards creating harmony in the relationship.

The Need to Be Heard

This may sound like a strange need but it is actually an important one. Men receive a lot of credibility in their own minds by having other people listen to their opinions and thoughts. As his partner he needs you to listen to him, encourage him and praise him when he comes up with a good idea. Acceptance is very important to the male. That is why the man is so macho about providing for his family, makes him feel appreciated and wanted; all important needs for a man. This goes both ways of course. Women also need to be heard but we forget sometimes that men need it just as much.

When a man is feeling like he has failed he may not be able to articulate his feels, mainly because he doesn't know how to. Expressing his feelings verbally can be difficult for a man; not impossible, but difficult. As his partner look for the signs on his face and in his body movements that tell you he is trying to say something that he needs to be heard. Through time and patience you will learn to recognize those traits in him and you will be able to respond accordingly.

His partner needs to be open to the man sharing his way and in his time. It is not as verbose as women are when it comes to sharing. Two women can meet for coffee and talk for hours at a time. Two men meet for coffee and they are finished in fifteen minutes. In those fifteen minutes though each man can have communicated enough information to keep the other satisfied that he knows everything about his buddy. A woman needs to understand this about a man. He doesn't share a lot verbally with men either; it is not just women he doesn't verbalize with. But, and this is a big but, he does communicate a lot in actions and movements. A slap on the back, a nudge in the side; these kinds of communications say a lot to men from men. It says I care, I understand, I am here for you. A man can't go around slapping his partner on the back or nudging her in the side, she might slap him up the side of the head.

Just accept the fact that men communicate differently but they do need to be heard. They need to know that their partner cares enough about them to take the time to listen to them in their way. It might sound tough but you can do it ladies; I know you can.

The Need for Intimacy

I know what you are thinking ladies; sex is not intimacy. Pardon me for saying so but it is very intimate and it does have emotional consequences for the man even if he does not realize it at the time. Men like physical contact with a woman. The need for sex is great in a man. He has to learn to harness that with his emotions so that sex is also an emotional thing. Keeping sex from a man in a relationship is not going to help him be more emotional. In fact, it will have the opposite effect; he will withdraw and become moody. Because he gets a lot of his self-esteem from pleasing his partner physically when this doesn't happen he feels rejected and a failure

Because a man gets a lot of emotional satisfaction from sex it is very important to him. His feeling of accomplishment and success as a lover build his self-esteem. Praise for his lovemaking skills from his partner is very important to him. If he has satisfied her physically he naturally assumes he has satisfied her emotionally because he is satisfied emotionally. He has to learn, and ladies, you have to help the men with this, that emotional fulfillment for a woman is different than it is for a man. She needs to be told she is loved, appreciated, wanted, and that she satisfies him physically more than any other woman could. Helping your male partner understand this will go a long way towards helping him learn.

Ask a man pointed questions. Instead of asking him if he loves you ask him what feelings he has inside of him when he thinks of you. Words like love, commitment, marriage, and the like scare a man because he is afraid of such things. He doesn't want to get hurt so he steers away from those words. If you ask him what are his long-term goals for life; what makes him truly happy every day, where does he see the two of you in ten years? Questions like these will get a much better answer from him and help him to be clear in his thinking and explanations. Women just have to learn how to phrase a question to get the answer they really want. That is why women have to understand that asking a man the same question you ask a woman will not get the same kind of answer. Men are analytical. They analyze and dissect issues and problems. Women deal with problems head on; they want to get them resolved immediately. No messing around. Men have to ponder an issue, quietly, before they can start trying to resolve it. Example. The screen door needs fixing. You tell him the problem and assume it will be taken care of immediately. He on the other hand has to analyze the best way to deal with the problem and it may get put on the back burner. Solution. Here is what you say to the man.

Honey, I am going to Home Depot. What supplies would you like me to pick up to fix the screen door? Either he will be thrilled and tell you what he needs or he will panic and say he will go with you to get the supplies which is his way of saying he doesn't trust you to get the right stuff. Either way you win. You get the supplies and now the problem must be resolved because you have created the solution for him. That is a lot easier and more productive than nagging him to fix the screen door. Does that help ladies? I hope so. You can apply this principle to every situation you come up with. Don't ask him a direct question; phrase your thoughts in such a way as to give him no option but to answer. I am sure you will get good at it and your life will be a lot easier.

Relationship Advice

EFFECT OF SEX ON RELATIONSHIP

Talking About Sex - Exploring Sexuality With Kindness and Compassion

Sex, the most intimate, layered, and loaded of topics. Few subjects are more personal or individual. Sexuality is a complex composite of culture, gender, beliefs inherited from our families, life experiences, biology, etc. It is as unique to an individual as their finger prints. And so it follows that exposing your sexual fears and desires can feel incredibly vulnerable. As terrifying as this process might be, however, learning to communicate openly, respectfully, and continuously about sex can improve your sex life ten-fold, deepen your relationship with your partner and yourself, help you to feel more comfortable in and loving towards your own body, and enhance your appreciation and understanding of your own sexuality. Let's look at how you can facilitate a healthy, mutually-beneficial dialogue about sex with your partner.

Know what you bring to the table...

What does sex mean for you? Consider who you are as a sexual being. What emotions does the idea of discussing your sexual desires bring up for you? Fear? Excitement? Shame? Let your feelings arise without judgment. Think back on your past sexual experiences. How did you feel about yourself? Are there aspects of these experiences you would like to create with your current partner? What helps you to feel safe and relaxed with a sexual partner? How important is sex to you? Is sex more of an emotional act or a physical act for you? The idea here is to begin to explore and embrace your sexuality from a place of allowance.

Where are your boundaries? Most people have at least a few sexual frontiers they would rather not explore. Be candid with yourself about what makes you uncomfortable and be willing to assert those boundaries with your partner.

What does your ideal sex life look like? You are far more likely to get what you want when you ask for it. Spend some time thinking about what your ideal sex life might look like. How often would you like to have sex? How important to you is emotional intimacy, foreplay, variety, monogamy?

Set the stage...

Pick a stress-free time in a private place. Creating a relaxed, secure environment is essential when discussing a subject as sacred and personal as sexuality. Schedule a time when you will not be rushed or interrupted. Choose a secluded venue which allows you to speak freely.

Check-in with one another. Take a moment to check-in with where you are both at emotionally. Knowing that one or both of you are entering into the conversation tired, distracted, anxious, etc. can help to mitigate the impact of those preexisting states. You may also want to check-out before ending the conversation.

Establish some guidelines for communication. What do each of you need in order for this conversation to feel safe, loving, and inviting? Discuss confidentiality explicitly. If you are not comfortable having the details of your discussion shared with friends or loved ones, make that clear from the outset. Bringing an overall attitude of goodwill is paramount to the success of any dialogue about sex. Some general rules which help foster goodwill might be; no blaming or degrading language, describe what you would like but don't demand it, and both participants have the right to end the conversation (with an agreed upon time to resume it) at any time.

Cultivate effective communication...

Employ respect and kindness. Use "I" statements. This does not mean, "I feel like you are a jerk". It means taking ownership of your own emotional experience, not attributing it to your partner's actions. For example, "I notice that sex often brings up feelings of insecurity for me" is different than, "you always make me feel insecure during sex". Practice emotional responsibility, it will keep your partner off the defense and allow you to be confident in your integrity. Be aware of your emotions and conscientious of how your partner is feeling. Express your fears and concerns. Respect each other's boundaries.

Talk as a team. Approach this discussion as a collaborative effort not a conflict in which you are on opposing sides. You both have the same goal. Work together, as a unified force, to accomplish your shared goal.

Avoid communication missteps. Denying/avoiding, intellectualizing, minimizing, defending/justifying, deflecting, catastrophizing/dramatizing, assuming, dredging up the past, threatening, attacking, discounting, interrupting, generalizing, preaching, and feigning agreement. These are only a few of the ways in which people fail to hear and acknowledge the feelings of others. Give some thought to which of these you are most guilty and begin to be more conscious of how that affects your relationships.

Move from talk to touch...

Take it to the bedroom. Once you have come to an agreement about some elements you would like to change, experiment with, or add to your sexual repertoire, move the discussion to the bedroom. Add a sensate component to your conversation. Explore how you each like to be touched, talked to, seen. This is a trust building exercise so be gentle with each other.

Keep it light. Too much pressure can take the sexy right out of a situation. Let this be a fun, light adventure into exploring and discovering things about your partner. Laugh at yourselves, be playful, and enjoy the intimacy of being safe while vulnerable together.

Maintain your gains...

Make time for sex. That doesn't mean every Wednesday at 5:45. Scheduling time for sex and intimacy can feel sterile and overly structured, but forgetting to make sex a priority altogether can be even more detrimental. Make time for sex, and even more importantly, for connecting with your partner, just as you make time for exercise, regular meals, and sleep. Sexual intimacy is a vital part of a satisfying relationship.

One question a week. Make sex an ongoing topic of discussion. Now that the lines of communication are open, keep them that way! One way to keep sex out from under the rug is to integrate a weekly sex question into your discussions. Here are a few examples:

How does your mood impact our sex life, your desire for sex, etc.?

What are you embarrassed to ask for during sex?

What is the most important part of sex for you?

What is your favorite part of my body? Of your body?

Are there any sexual fantasies you would enjoy playing out together?

How can I show you that I am interested in sex?

Creating a space where you are free to express your sexuality openly and without judgment is a very healing and liberating experience. Being ridiculed or shamed, however, can be scarring. As the old adage instructs, do unto others as you would have them do unto you. Showing kindness, respect, and reverence for your partner's sexuality creates the fertile soil in which a healthy and satisfying sexual relationship can grow.

Relationship Advice

Relationship Advice

CPSIA information can be obtained
at www.ICGtesting.com
Printed in the USA
BVHW010741060521
606332BV00025B/1430